The Craftsman's Art Series

The Craft of
Dressmaking

Ann Ladbury

Stanley Paul, London

Illustrations and section on designing
by Beryl Rouse

Stanley Paul & Co Ltd
3 Fitzroy Square, London W1

An imprint of the Hutchinson Publishing Group

London Melbourne Sydney Auckland
Wellington Johannesburg and agencies
throughout the world

First published 1976
Second impression June 1976
Third impression May 1977
© Ann Ladbury 1976
Illustrations © Stanley Paul & Co Ltd 1976

Printed in Great Britain by litho by The Anchor Press Ltd
and bound by Wm Brendon & Son Ltd
both of Tiptree, Essex

ISBN 0 09 124680 6 (cased)
       0 09 124681 4 (paperback)

Contents

Introduction

This is a sewing book for beginners; for those who would like to sew but are not sure where, or how, to start. Although this is a practical book to be used while sewing, nevertheless it can be used as a reference book for checking odd points. Also, if you are an absolute beginner it will be a help to read the book right through first to get a general idea of what is going to be really important once you start.

I have taken it for granted that you want to start making clothes either for economy or as a creative interest but that you have little or no experience, perhaps only a couple of failures, behind you. Once you have made a few simple garments using the book in conjunction with the pattern, you will be feeling more confident and will be able to progress to more difficult things.

The book is also for those with some experience. Pattern instruction sheets take it for granted that you can sew. They give you an order of making that particular garment but they are not intended as complete instructions on exactly how to do the processes. This book is intended to be used as an adjunct to the paper pattern and its instructions, and I have included all the vital basic processes necessary for making fairly easy clothes.

I have left out all the more difficult areas of sewing because if the beginner tackles them she is almost bound to fail and this will discourage her. She may have wasted money and this will put her off, no matter how determined and brave she was to start with. A good finish can be achieved on all the processes included in the book if you follow the instructions closely. If you are experienced already, then the chapters on making a start, shopping, and buying a sewing machine can be skipped, as the information will already be familiar to you.

My own philosophy of dressmaking is that if you really want a hand-made (not home-made!) finish you have got to pay attention to preparation (including correct choice of pattern and fabric) to fitting and to pressing; this last being perhaps the most important of all.

It is only with practice that you will gradually acquire skill in all three and so begin to produce well-finished garments, and that is why I have dealt with these three aspects in particular detail.

Explanations have been kept as uncomplicated as possible but there are several terms which may need clarifying.

FITTING LINE.   The dotted line within the pattern edge; this is the line on which you should stitch after cutting out.

TACK AND BASTE.   These are both temporary stitches which are removed after machining has been done. Tacking is a straight stitch between $\frac{1}{2}$ in/13 mm and 2 in/5 cm long. Basting is a diagonal tacking worked in rows and covering a bigger area. Stitches are normally larger than for tacking.

GRAIN.   This is the straight thread of the fabric, either down or across the material.

NAP.   This really means 'pile' on a fabric which makes it necessary to cut all pieces lying in one direction to avoid shading. However, when 'nap' is mentioned on the yardage chart on a pattern envelope you can take it to mean any one-way fabric whether with a pile or simply a one-way print.

PROCESSES.   Construction of a garment is composed of processes, and the selection of processes varies with the garment. A process is a complete piece of construction in itself; for example, hem, button-hole, collar.
Throughout the book I use the following abbreviations:

  CB and CF to denote centre back and centre front.
  RS and WS to denote right side and wrong side of the work.

One-way fabrics are any which have a pile or nap and also those whose design is applied in one direction only. Examine the fabric closely before purchase as you will need to buy more if it is one-way. Nearly all fabrics are printed one-way, although with some prints the difference is so slight that you can ignore it. Check fabrics too are nearly always one-way.

1. Buying a Sewing Machine

This is a little like buying a car – you only look at the models you know you can afford; there is no point in hankering after the others way beyond your pocket. Nor should you complain later that you do not possess the refinements of those other models, because, although you do get what you pay for, you only get what you pay for and no more. But do buy the best you can afford at the time.

Go to your local sewing-machine shop and have a look at what is available to get an idea of prices, then go home and decide what you can afford. It is worth consulting the issues of *Which?* that have covered sewing machines, as these will tell you a lot more than the brochures. Most shops offer discounts, so it is worthwhile going for the biggest.

Go to the shop and ask to see some machines working. Come to terms with the amount of use the machine will have. If you already have a home, family and full-time job you are unlikely to be able to make justifiable use of a fully automatic model. You will be shown semi-automatics and fully automatics. Obviously both still need help from you, but whereas the semi-automatics have manual adjustments to be made and a limited range of stitches, fully automatics have everything built-in, so all you do is turn a knob or flick a switch. These incorporate a wide range of stitches. All machines do straight stitch, but it is almost essential now to buy a swing-needle machine; that is, one that will do zigzag stitch, because so many fabrics fray and have to be neatened. No one has the time now to neaten everything by hand, and in any case, many synthetic fibres are so slippery that it is difficult to contain the fraying with a hand stitch. So many fabrics are knitted too and it is vital to be able to sew them with a slight zigzag stitch, to avoid puckering, especially on the light-weight ones. It is a boon, too, to be able to do buttonholes by machine. Although obviously on some garments it is desirable to make the buttonholes by another method, if you can do them by machine at least you can tackle blouses and skirts and button-through dresses, and it is useful to be able to do them in awkward places such as cuffs and skirt or trouser waistbands.

Even the cheapest zigzag machines will also offer other stitches that might appeal to you: tacking, tailor tacking, blind hemming, and so on. As for the embroidery stitches available on many models, only you can decide what will be useful to you.

Look also for simplicity of threading and feet that are easy to change. Remember to lift the machine to make sure you will be able to carry it. Portability may be an important factor, especially if you are a student. If this is so, ask to see how it fits into its carrying case (some are extraordinarily difficult to put away) and carry it yourself.

Ask about the guarantee, about servicing, maintenance and spare parts. Provided you do not choose an obscure make there is no problem in this country with maintaining foreign machines. Every town has a general sewing-machine shop which stocks the main makes.

Care of the machine

Machines like being used provided they are well cared for. Clean it often, clearing out fluff after every garment, and put one drop of oil in all the oil points fairly often.

Learning to use the machine

If you have not used a machine before, begin by practising on sheets of lined paper. Do not thread up the machine, but learn to follow straight lines and turn corners and work curves. Also, practise machining slowly. This requires much more skill than fast stitching. Mark a few points on the paper and practise starting and stopping exactly on these points. Finally, when you are in complete control, thread up and practise on fabric, remembering to stitch on double fabric which represents the thickness you will be working on with garments.

Straight-edge stitching

Use the edge of the foot or one of the grooves as a guide for keeping edge-stitching straight. Keep your eye on that part of the foot as you sew and not on the needle.

A good free-arm machine

Zigzag stitching for neatening

A big zigzag will not prevent fraying. Use the shortest closest stitch that you can, according to your fabric. Stitch in the correct direction (see next section) otherwise zigzag stitch can cause even more fraying.

Gathering threads

Set the machine to the longest straight stitch and work on the right side of the fabric. Lower foot on to fabric, reverse for a few stitches to fasten the end off, and then machine to the point where the gathers are to end. Do not fasten off; leave long ends to pull gathers up. For smooth, even gathers work two rows of machining $\frac{1}{4}$ in/6 mm apart.

Pin the gathered section to the part it is to join and then pull up the gathers to fit, taking hold of the ends of thread on the wrong side of the fabric. These are the threads that came off the spool as you stitched.

When things go wrong

If your machine fails to stitch or stitches badly, unthread it and start again. Check the spool and insert it again. Test the stitch on a spare piece of folded fabric. If it is still not correct, try a different-sized needle and a different length of stitch. Apparently over 90 per cent of sewing machine problems are due to needle or thread and not to the machine. It can be quite tricky to obtain a good stitch on some new fabrics, but persevere with threading and different needles. A piece of fluff, a blunt needle, or a needle that is too small or too big, is often enough to prevent the machine from stitching.

Consult your machine handbook if you continually have trouble with a particular fabric.

2. Shopping

You will be shopping for pattern, fabric and haberdashery, in that order, and it makes it a bit easier if you can go to a department store or a shop that stocks all three, so that you can buy everything at once. It helps to have a clear, but not rigid, idea of what you are going to make, otherwise the pattern catalogues may confuse you. If there is a 'Very Easy' or 'Easy to Make' section, turn to that first as these will show the simpler styles.

Choosing a pattern style

Keep to simple styles at first with few processes. Give yourself a chance to come to terms with your equipment before attempting complicated, time-consuming processes.

A simple, raglan-sleeved, wrap-over housecoat is an excellent way to begin, as you only have seams and edges to tackle. Your next garment can add one process; it could be, for instance, a simple tabard, or long wrap-round skirt. On the next garment you can progress and add one more process and so on to gain experience without tackling too much at once. The difficult processes are collars, buttonholes, cuffs, and setting in sleeves, so avoid these for a while. Also avoid, at all costs, the 'simple shirtwaister' dress because it is far from simple. Remember that children's clothes are just as difficult, with the processes the same but on a smaller scale, but children are not as fussy about the fit or the finish.

Size

The main adult categories in the pattern catalogues are as follows:

Misses: For the average, well-proportioned figure of 5 ft 5 in. – 5 ft 6 in./1·65 m – 1·68 m tall.

Miss Petite: For the shorter, but well-proportioned 'Miss' figure with short back neck to waist measurement.

Women's: For the bigger woman, fully developed and taller. These patterns usually start at size 42 in./107 cm bust.

Half Size: For the shorter, thicker-waisted, mature figure with short back neck to waist measurement. The bust sizes run from 33–47 in./84–119 cm, and from bust 43 in./109 cm the difference between the bust and hip measurement also increases.

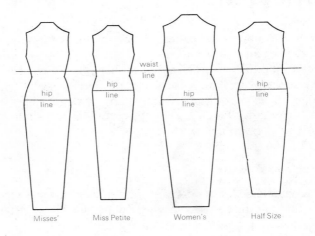

The diagram gives you an approximate idea of the relative proportions of the various ranges, but in the back of each pattern catalogue you will find details of the measurements of the patterns in each category. Choose the pattern which conforms most closely to your measurements, buying where possible to your bust size, as this is a more difficult area to alter than waist, hip or length. Remember that if you are less than 5 ft 4 in./1·63 m tall and short-waisted, either the Miss Petite or Half Size patterns are likely to need less alteration for your figure than Misses' or Women's.

Taking your measurements

Make sure you are familiar with your measurements before going to buy a pattern. Find someone to take the four basic measurements you need and measure as follows, over normal foundation garments.

1. *Bust.* Run the tape over the fullest part of the bust meeting the tape between the shoulder blades at the back. There is a lot of movement here, so do not take a tight measurement.

2. *Waist.* Take a firm measurement round the smallest part. Those with small waists usually like it quite tight, while those who tend to expand and contract will prefer a loose measurement.

3. *Hips.* This is the most difficult measurement to take because it is not easy to determine where the hips are. The position can be anywhere between 5 in./12·5 cm and 9 in./23 cm below the waist according to the body proportions. A woman who is tall may have long legs and very high hip bones, and a short woman can have low hips. Feel the pelvic bone at the side of the figure and take the measurement where the bone sticks out furthest. Many women have an indentation below this which is emphasized by corsets and pantie-girdles. The hip measurement is always above this and above crotch level. Take the measurement firmly and level all round. This may not be the widest part of your figure as you may have big thighs or big low buttocks. If this is so you need to take another measurement at that level, not to consider when buying the pattern, but in order to check the width of pattern at that point later.

4. *Back neck to waist.* Tie a tape or string round your waist and measure from the base of the neck, or where top vertebra protrudes, down to lower edge of tape or string.

Checking and altering the pattern

Before cutting out check the length of each piece against your measurements and lengthen or shorten if necessary. There are lines on most patterns to indicate where the alterations should be made.

1. *Back neck to waistline.* Compare with your own measurement and lengthen the pattern by cutting and opening, or shorten by pleating, between waist and underarm. Alter front and back.

2. *Hip Level.* The pattern will have been designed with the hipline

at 9 in./23 cm below the waist for Misses' and Women's, 7 in./18 cm for Half Size and Miss Petite. If you took your measurements higher than this then make a pleat across the front and back skirt pattern to lift hip line.

3. *Sleeve Length.*   Measure an existing sleeve seam and compare with the pattern, lengthen or shorten on the lines shown.

4. *Thighs.*   If your thigh measurement is larger than it should be, check the width of the two pattern pieces combined, at the level you took the measurement and add at least 2 in./5 cm for ease. If it is not enough, remember to add some on the seams when cutting out. This can be run out gradually from the hip level.

Choosing the fabric

On the back of the pattern envelope will be a chart giving the amount of material you need to buy, according to its width. In addition some patterns will give a list of suggested fabrics. If so, be guided by the list. If the pattern suggests soft fabrics and you buy something stiff, your result will probably be very disappointing.

Go to the fabric department clutching your pattern and start to look round. You will probably already have some idea of the colours you prefer and something will catch your eye. Feel the fabrics you like and crush a small corner in your hand to see if it creases. Beware if it springs up too readily when you open your hand because this is how it will behave in use making it difficult to 'ease' on collars or facings. For early garments choose medium-weight materials such as brushed rayon, Viyella, soft cottons, seersucker, nylon or polyester jersey. Avoid light-weight fabrics such as chiffon or georgette or anything you can see through, and avoid all heavy fabrics such as suiting, gaberdine, coatings and fur fabrics. Choose a plain fabric or an all-over print, avoiding large one-way designs and checks.

Sort out two or three rolls of fabric and go to a mirror. Drape each one over you, near your face, to see which colour suits you best, and also drape the fabric somewhat in the style of the pattern; for instance if the pattern has gathers bunch the fabric up to see if it falls and drapes well.

If the sales assistant appears to be interested and co-operative ask her opinion about the suitability of the fabric for the style. Buy only the amount stated on the pattern. There is no need to buy an extra ¼ yd/23 cm 'just in case'. If you work slowly and carefully nothing will go wrong, even at the cutting-out stage, and even if you do make some dreadful error it is unlikely that the extra $\frac{1}{4}$ yd/23 cm will be sufficient to correct it.

Haberdashery

On the back of the pattern envelope will be a list of the haberdashery you will need to make that garment. The list will include:

1. Thread. It is simplest to buy an all-purpose thread such as Coats' Drima, then you needn't worry about matching up to the fibre content of your fabric.

2. Interfacing. Interfacing is used to reinforce selected areas like collars and cuffs. Buy a light-weight interfacing such as Vilene. Ask the assistant's advice if you are unsure of the correct weight, but test it by wrapping the fabric round the interfacing and feeling it. It should not feel too stiff: ideally it should make the material slightly more rigid without changing its character too drastically. Many different types are available in woven and non-woven materials. A non-woven interfacing like Vilene is easier to handle. It has no grain and does not fray.

3. Zip. If a zip is used the pattern will tell you the length, choose one with nylon teeth for medium- or light-weight fabrics.

4. Other items such as hooks, press studs, elastic will also be listed.

Equipment

In addition you will need other items of sewing equipment, some of which you may already have, but if not you can buy them in the store while buying the haberdashery.

1. Needles. A packet of assorted sizes. The 'Betweens' type are best as they are short.

2. Pins. A box of good-quality steel pins.

3. Thimble. A tailor's thimble which has no top is the most comfortable.

4. Chalk. A piece of tailor's chalk in white.

5. Beeswax. For waxing double thread for strength.

6. Scissors. Three pairs are eventually necessary: a small pair for

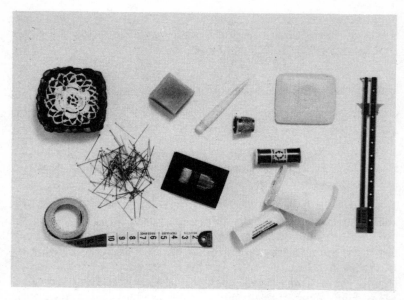

Hand-sewing equipment

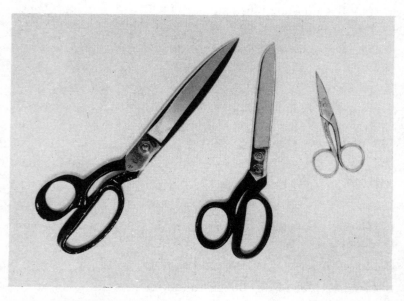

The three sizes of scissors

snipping threads, but not so small that they are uncomfortable to hold (not embroidery scissors); a medium pair with blades about 6 in/15 cm long, and a very large pair of shears for cutting out.

7. *A hem marker and a metal adjustable marker are optional.*

8. *Tape measure and ruler.*

There are some short cuts you can take, using aids to sewing, which will make it easier but not lower the standard of finish. These include:

'Velcro'.   The touch and close fastener which grips firmly. Use in place of conventional fastenings. Sew on by hand or machine. Sold in pre-packs and cut lengths.

Wundaweb.   A fine web which, when placed between two layers of fabric and pressed, melts and joins the layers. Marvellous in hems and for holding facings in place. Use a medium-hot iron over a damp cloth, or a steam iron and press several times to make sure the web melts. Available in pre-packs, both small and a large economy pack.

Bondaweb.   This is like Wundaweb but has paper on the back which you tear off after applying. Helps to prevent fraying and also bonds layers together. Use in buttonholes, bottom of openings, corners of collars; slip a piece in anywhere the fabric is being cut and may be likely to fray later. Available in pre-packs.

Vilene and other non-woven interfacings are easy to use as they do not fray. They are either iron-on or sew-in and available in a variety of weights to suit the fabric you are using. Sold by the yard/metre, or in packs.

Press studs in strips.   If you have a lot to sew on you can buy a tape with press studs attached. Sew on by hand. Only use where there is no danger of it showing as the tape is only either black or white.

Press fasteners with tops.   You can buy packets of fasteners with fancy metal caps. Some are attached with a tool, some with a tap of the hammer. They fasten like press studs but look like buttons from the outside.

3. Making a Start

Some parts of this process may appear fiddly but doing them correctly will pay dividends later on.

Preparing the pattern

1. Identify the version you are making and mark it on the envelope.
2. Take out the instruction sheet and locate the area showing the shapes and numbers of all the pattern pieces.
3. Next find the layout diagram that applies to your version *and* your fabric. Circle it with a pen.
4. Look at layout diagram and see which numbers of pattern pieces are used. Tick them off on the numbered pattern shapes above.
5. Remove pattern from envelope. Go through all pieces and put aside those not required by you. If some are together on one sheet cut off the ones not required.
6. Put pieces not required into polythene bag, not back into the envelope.
7. Using old scissors or a pair kept for paper cutting, trim all pieces on the thick outer line, often labelled 'cutting line'. Ignore the diamond-shaped balance marks, cut straight past them.
8. Run a cool iron over all pieces.

If this is your first garment this may well be enough for your first session.

Note: When you have finished with the pattern, fold the pieces and put in the polythene bag with the pattern envelope and store. You will find it very frustrating to try and replace the pattern in its envelope.

ADJUST THE PATTERN. See Fitting, page 42.

Preparing the fabric

1. Press the length of fabric. If using a steam iron it should be safe to press on the right side; if using an ordinary iron it will be advisable to test for temperature on a small corner and then press on WS.

2. Fabric now has to be straightened at one end. If the fabric was torn off the roll at the shop, then that end will already be on the straight thread. If it was cut, then you must straighten it as follows:

Knitted fabrics

Trace a row of knitting across the width and draw a chalk line to follow it. This may be difficult to see on a plain fabric, but if it is a jacquard you will be able to follow the pattern.

Plain woven fabrics

Lift up one thread with a pin and pull it gently. There is no need to remove it completely, simply dislodging it will make an obvious straight line across the fabric.

Cut the end on the straight grain if this does not lose too much of your fabric on one side, which you may need later, or mark the line with chalk and when the fabric is folded pin the layers together on this line (a).

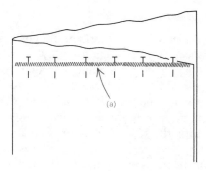

(a)

Printed fabrics, checked fabrics or those with large patterns

At this stage of your experience you shouldn't be using checks or large patterns at all, but it may be that you are using up an old length as an experiment or a try-out before making up the garment properly.

Check fabric, or any other with a definite straight line such as spots or stripes, must be cut on the line of the pattern, regardless of grain. It often happens with printed spots, for instance, that the printing is crooked and in this case you must ignore the straight grain or the effect will be wrong.

Large-patterned prints should be handled in the same way, working to place the printed pattern evenly on the garment and ignoring the straight threads. It is very unlikely except with a very expensive print that trouble has been taken to ensure that it is straight on the threads.

Small all-over prints can be treated as plain fabric.

One-way fabrics: Most prints will have a one-way design, so examine the fabric to see if this is so. In addition, jersey or knitted fabrics are best cut with the pattern pieces in one direction because the knitting process is done in one direction and this can cause shading if some pieces are upside down. One-way designs take more fabric, see below.

Fold and lay out the fabric

Follow the diagram on the instruction sheet. This will tell you how to fold and lay the material. Lay with RS up so that you can clearly see the pattern and any flaws.

Pinning down the pattern

Place the prepared pieces on the fabric in the positions indicated on the instruction sheet, laying them roughly in position. If your table or cutting board is not big enough to take the whole length, put one pin in the middle of each pattern piece to hold it in place, then roll up that area while you work on the next section.

Remember that if your fabric is one-way only, then all pieces must be placed with the top edge or neck in one direction. This will mean adjusting the positions of the pieces slightly. Dovetail the pieces in order to be as economical as possible.

After satisfying yourself that all pieces will fit on to fabric, begin to pin firmly.

Rules for pinning:

(a) Use as few pins as possible.

(b) Place them well *within* the seam lines of the pattern. (If put round the edge they cause lifting and uneven edge.)

(c) Insert pins diagonally; that is on the bias of the fabric where it will give slightly (b). Putting pins *with* the straight grain will cause puckering.

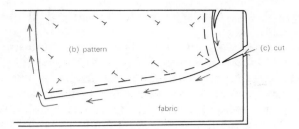

Cutting out

1. Use large scissors and cut with blades to left of pattern edge, leaning blades slightly towards the pinned pattern piece (c). Many people advocate cutting the other side and using one hand to hold the pattern down, but in fact the former method does not lift the pattern at all and also your eye is directly above the scissors which makes your cutting more accurate.

2. Cut with long strokes, opening the scissors as far down as you comfortably can, and then cutting right to the points.

3. Move scissors forward, check that when open again they fit exactly into previous cut, to avoid a chopped edge.

4. Cut out the main pattern pieces only. Cutting out is quite a nerve-racking experience for beginners and it is daunting to be confronted by a big pile of pieces. Cut only the back and the front or the main pieces to be assembled first. There is no need to cut sleeves yet and it is best not to cut small pieces such as collars or facings in case they get lost.

5. Ignore the triangle-shaped balance marks, cut straight past them.

6. After cutting main pieces roll up remainder with pattern still pinned in place.

If this is your first garment this is probably enough for your second session.

Marking darts and turnings

Although this seems tedious at first, nevertheless you must have some indication on your cut material of where to put darts and seams.

The first method is the one you will probably prefer at first, but the second is the best and most professional.

Using a tracing wheel and dressmaker's carbon paper

The carbon paper can be bought at most haberdashery counters.

You may have to go to a large store for a tracing wheel. See Equipment, page 13.

1. It is easier to work with the carbon paper cut into strips 2 in./ 5 cm wide. Fold each strip with carbon outside and slide it between the two layers of fabric under the turning line. There should be no need to move any pins except perhaps where darts occur.

2. Work on a piece of hardboard or a cutting board, not on the dining table, and run the tracing wheel firmly along the seam lines and darts. You can also mark other points such as position of gathers.

3. Remove paper. Unpin pattern and you will find the turnings marked on the WS of both halves of the fabric.

Tailor tacking

This may appear to take longer than carbon paper at first, but as you become more accustomed to sewing you will prefer this method because it marks both sides of the fabric and the threads are removed immediately. As the fabric is still flat on the table, this is a very accurate mark, so it helps to leave the tailor tacks in as a guide when machining.

1. Fold back the pattern tissue on the seam line, snipping the paper where curves appear and cutting up one line of darts (through paper only) and folding them back (d).

2. Thread a needle, size 5 or 6, with a long piece of tacking thread and pull it through double. Do not knot the end.

3. Work round the edge of pattern, taking stitches beside folded paper. Pick up a bare $\frac{1}{4}$ in./6 mm or less of fabric, but leave a stitch on the surface of 1 in./2·5 cm or more, 2 in./5 cm on long straight edges. Do not leave loops and do not make double stitches.

4. End threads by cutting off and start new thread at next stitch. Mark darts, etc., in the same way, working up each side and placing one stitch at the point (e).

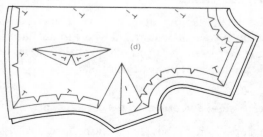

5. Unpin pattern pieces.

6. Snip loops of thread on surface of fabric (f).

7. Carefully part the two layers of fabric and as soon as threads show snip again (g). Take care not to snip material as well.

You will now have two parts of garment accurately marked on both sides.

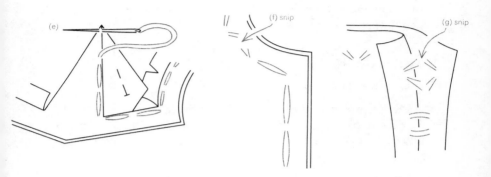

Reasons for tailor tacks falling out

1. You are not using proper tacking thread, which is deliberately made slightly hairy so that it grips the fabric.

2. The needle is too big and so is making a hole bigger than the thread.

3. You are picking up too much fabric on the needle so that instead of jamming the fabric in as a V, you are leaving a loop on the underside as well.

4. The stitches on the surface are too long and you are therefore catching the long ends in your fingers and pulling them out as you work.

Before folding and putting away, run the iron over the pattern to smooth out the turnings.

Interfacing

You will have bought this when buying the fabric, see Shopping, page 13. Now is the time to decide, before pieces of fabric are handled, where to put it.

Your pattern will guide you as to the obvious positions such as collars and cuffs which you will deal with later in the construction, but the basic rule for the use of interfacing, such as Vilene, is that it should go into any section of the garment that will be subjected to strain, or any area that needs to be kept crisp. It is often advisable, for instance, to interface a yoke area in medium or heavy fabrics. It is always necessary to interface a neckline, except where there is a collar, because it supports the whole weight of the garment.

Follow the pattern, cutting interfacing as instructed and after the experience of a few garments, start making your own decisions about where else to use it.

Attaching interfacing

Iron-on varieties

Ascertain which is the sticky side and place down to WS fabric. Insert one pin. Repeat on all pieces. Press in position, remove pin, and continue to press until it adheres. Plonk the iron, never slide it.

Sew-in varieties

Place to WS fabric and baste in position, keep work flat on the table (h).

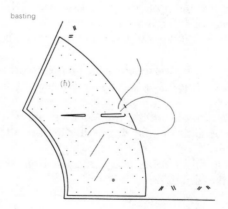

With both types you now make up the garment, trimming away edges of interfacing later where possible to reduce bulk.

Assembling the garment for fitting

1. Put in any shaping such as darts, gathering threads and tack.

2. Tack side seams, centre front and centre back seams and shoulders. Tacking should be worked with both edges of fabric towards you, flat on the table. Use a knot and do not make stitches too large. See Darts, page 31, and Seams, page 23.

3. If the garment is a dress with centre back opening you will find fitting easier if you close this seam right up with tacking and leave open part of the left-side seam instead, and also the left shoulder seam.

4. Fit the garment. See Fitting, page 42. Unpick seam tacking and machine and finish darts. Re-tack main seams and stitch and finish.

Having reached this stage you are now ready to cut out the pieces needed for the next process shown on your instruction sheet, but read the following sections in the book on Processes, for hints on the easiest ways of tackling them.

4. Seams

Seams are used for joining together the pieces of material that are to make the garment.

The three types of seam most commonly used are the open or plain seam, French seam and welt or double-stitched seam. The open seam can be used on all garments but choice will depend on the material you are handling and the effect you want.

Choice of seam

TABLE I

Type	Advantages	Fabrics and Garments	Disadvantages
1. OPEN	Inconspicuous; flat; neat, tailored appearance.	All fabrics except fine badly fraying ones such as chiffon. Suitable for all garments.	Turnings can form ridge which shows on right side. Hole is obvious if seam splits.
2. FRENCH	Encloses raw edges on fine fabrics; narrow, so on transparent materials will not show an ugly width of double fabric. Two rows of stitching so a split seam will not be immediately obvious.	Use only on thin fraying materials, e.g. voile, chiffon, georgette, cotton batiste. Garments will therefore include blouses, some evening dresses, nightwear, underwear.	Too bulky to use on medium or heavy fabrics. Difficult to obtain even seam. Due to the fact that edges have to be enclosed the first row of stitching is worked a little way away from the fitting line and not on it.
3. WELT	Flat; strong, either side can be used as the right side except when used on coats. Two rows of stitching are used so it is unlikely to split in wear.	Any medium-weight or coat-weight fabric fraying or non-fraying. Any garment where the stitching adds to the general appearance. Most attractive when used on denim, sailcloth, poplin, twill. Useful on coats and reversible cloth but needs slightly different treatment, see instructions below.	Unattractive on floral or dainty fabrics or luxury garments. Keep it as a utility seam.

How to sew an open seam

1. Place one piece of fabric on table right side uppermost.

2. Place second piece of fabric on top right side down. Raw edges should be towards you.

3. Tack on fitting line (a), do not stretch either piece and keep work flat on table while tacking.

4. Place under machine with bulk of fabric to left. Start at widest part of fabric. This will normally be hem, underarm or neck. (See page 30 for instructions on correct direction of stitching.)

5. Machine slowly a fraction beside tacks, slightly nearer to raw edge (b) but no more than the width of the machine needle. Try to see that top layer of fabric is eased under foot rather than stretched or a wrinkled seam will result. Stitching too fast will push top layer and cause the same problem.

6. Trim ends of thread, remove tacks carefully.

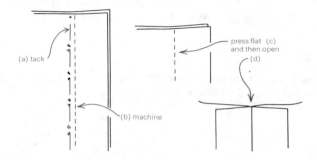

Pressing

Place seam flat on board, raw edges together and towards you. Press stitching flat to smooth out wrinkles and to help embed thread in fabric (c). Arrange so that you will be pressing in the same direction as you stitched. Open fabric over board ready to press stitching line down against board (d). Use toe of iron to open seam, then use about half the iron to press again, using pressing, not sliding, movements to avoid wrinkling the fabric. Finally press again with the whole of the iron. Turn work to RS and press again but more lightly, removing any wrinkles or pleats.

Neatening the raw edges of the open seam

This always seems an unnecessary chore to the beginner and in fact if you are using a completely firm, non-fraying material such as jersey, bonded fabric, flannel, then you need not neaten the edges. However, as you become more experienced you will realize how neatening improves the lie of the seam and the hang of the garment, and you will want to neaten all raw edges.

If you are using a fraying fabric you must neaten in order to prevent further fraying, because the movement of the body inside the garment will soon produce long threads hanging below the hem.

Method 1.   For machines that zigzag

Trim raw edges a little but do not reduce seam width to less than ½ in./13 mm or it may cause a ridge. Set machine to small zigzag width and short stitch. The bigger the zigzag and the longer the stitch, the less effective it will be in preventing fraying. Use a well-matching thread so that neatening is not obvious. Use this method on all except very fine, very fraying materials.

Pressing

Press each neatened edge separately, not against the garment, then re-press seam open, but lightly this time.

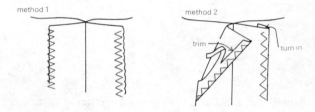

Method 2.   For machines that zigzag

Place edge to be neatened under machine with right side up. Turn under a small amount, ⅛ in./3 mm on fine fabrics, a little more on thicker fabrics such as brushed rayon. Set machine to small zigzag but a longer stitch than that described above because the stitch is to hold the edge, not prevent fraying. As you stitch turn under 3 in./7·5 cm or so of fabric at a time, stitch, stop, turn under again, stitch, and so on. The machine bed will hold the raw edge under and if you stretch the edge *slightly* you will obtain a good straight edge to machine on. Finish by turning to WS and trimming the raw edge close to the machining. Use medium scissors for trimming, not small ones that would produce a chopped edge.

Press each neatened edge separately after trimming. Re-press the seam open, but very lightly. If you find the neatening marks the garment slip a spare piece of the fabric under the edge and press again.

Method 3.   For straight-stitch machines

Set machine to the same length of stitch as used for the seam stitching. Place edge to be neatened under machine RS up, turn under a small amount and machine. The stitching should be right on the edge. It will take a little practice to machine right on the folded edge, but if you watch the needle you will soon be able to control it. Pull the edge *slightly* as you machine and this will give you a fold to follow. Turn under only a few inches at a time, do not try to do a long run.

Finish by trimming raw edges away on WS close to machining. Use medium-sized scissors.

Pressing

Press each edge separately, then press seam open again but lightly. If the neatening marks the garment place strips of the fabric under the edges and press again.

Method 4.   For straight-stitch machines

Place edge to be neatened under machine and, using the same stitch as for seams, work a row of straight stitching $\frac{1}{4}$ in./6 mm or so inside the raw edge. There is no need to measure this distance.

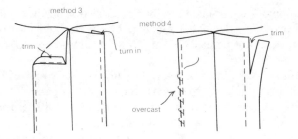

Use the edge of your machine foot as a guide, running it along raw edge.

Trim raw edge away close to machine stitching, a few inches at a time, and overcast by hand, from left to right, taking needle just below the machining and pulling thread tight. The machining does not prevent fraying, but the tight overcasting worked over the machined guide line will do so.

Pressing

Press each edge separately and then press seam open again, but lightly.

How to sew a French seam

1. Place one piece of fabric on table WS uppermost, raw edge towards you.
2. Place second piece of fabric WS down. Level up the edges and tack *on the fitting line* (a).

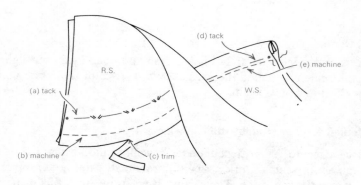

3. Place work under machine, lower foot so that needle is $\frac{1}{4}$ in./6 mm to the raw edge side of the tacking. Use your machine foot as a guide – it need not be exactly $\frac{1}{4}$ in/6 mm. Stitch in correct direction (b).
4. Remove tacks but not fitting line marks. Press row of stitching flat to remove wrinkles. Open work and carefully open the $\frac{1}{4}$ in/6 mm seam with the toe of the iron. Do not use the flat of the iron at all. Turn work over and press again, firmly this time.
5. Trim raw edges (c). The amount you cut off depends very much on the fabric, but as it must be fine and light-weight to use a French seam at all, you should be able to trim it down to about $\frac{1}{8}$ in./3 mm.
6. Working from WS of garment roll seam so that the join just pressed is right on the edge, tack, rolling with the fingers as you tack. The tacking need not be level or accurate but stitches must be below raw edges to prevent fraying appearing on RS garment (hold up to the light to see where they are) (d).

7. Press flat.

8. Place under machine and stitch, in correct direction, $\frac{1}{4}$ in./6 mm in from folded edge. Once again use your machine foot as the guide. This second row should be on the fitting line (e).

Pressing

Remove all tacks and press flat, then press towards back of garment lightly. Turn to right side and press again firmly.

How to sew a welt seam

This can be sewn with the right or wrong sides of the fabric together. I suggest you work a practice seam and decide which side you prefer as the right side. The instructions refer to the sort of seam used on men's shirts, where two rows of stitching are visible.

1. Place one piece of fabric WS uppermost on table, raw edges towards you.

2. Place second piece on top WS down. Tack on fitting line.

3. Machine, in correct direction, fractionally to one side, raw edge side, of the tacking (a).

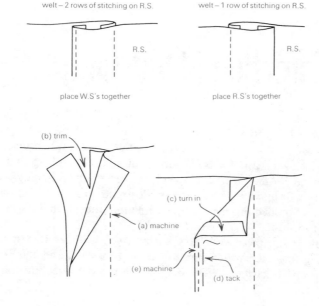

welt – 2 rows of stitching on R.S.

welt – 1 row of stitching on R.S.

R.S.

R.S.

place W.S's together

place R.S's together

(b) trim

(c) turn in

(a) machine

(e) machine

(d) tack

4. Remove tacks. Press seam stitching flat and then open fabric and press both raw edges towards one side. These edges are usually pressed towards the back of the garment.

5. Lift up the top one of the two raw edges, trim down the under one to $\frac{1}{4}$ in./6 mm or a little less if it does not fray, or if the fabric is thick (b).

6. Turn under the upper raw edge (c). Tack and press (d).

7. Machine, right on the edge, with a good straight stitch (e). Remove tacks.

Pressing

Press again, both sides.

Note: If using coat fabric or thick reversible fabric, you cannot turn under the edge at the second stage as it would be bulky and it is doubtful whether most machines would be able to take the thickness. The second row of stitching, therefore, is worked quite flat, an even distance (usually $\frac{3}{8}$ in./10 mm) from the edge. This leaves a raw edge which must be trimmed and this *must* be the inside of the garment, so it is essential to work a practice seam first.

5. Direction of Stitching

If you cut a piece of woven fabric at an angle and start to fray off the raw edge you will soon see that one set of threads come off more easily, and stick out, more than the others. When machining and pressing a seam it is best to machine so that you help that set of threads to lie flat, *with* them, not *against* them. Stitching against the fray will make it worse, it can also tend to stretch and wrinkle a seam. Stitched in the correct direction the garment will hang better too.

Look at the piece you have cut and you will see that it means stitching from the wider part to the narrow part, and this is what you do on all garments. The diagram shows the direction for most seams.

When you come to pressing and neatening (by hand or machine) the same rule applies.

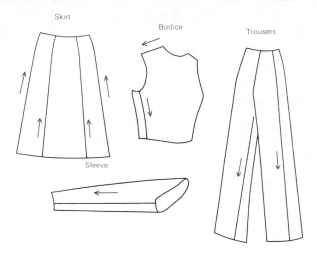

6. Darts

A dart is formed by folding the fabric and then stitching in a shaped line, either straight and at an angle, or, curved, or even with two pointed ends with a wider section between. Darts provide shaping for the various bulges of the figure to make the garment fit and to make it comfortable to wear. The stitching runs to a point and so a pocket of curved fabric appears in that position. Your aim is to make the shaping unobtrusive and to make it fit over the bulge concerned.

Where

Darts are used to accommodate busts, stomachs, buttocks, shoulder blades, Dowager's Humps (or round shoulders) and elbows. Shaping in other places is provided by curving the edge of the fabric so that it forms a bulge when joined to another piece – a dart in fact, but cut into the pieces of fabric.

Fit

To achieve a good fit you must move darts into the best position for you on the pattern before you cut out (see Fitting, page 42). When pressed the bulk of the fabric should lie towards the centre or towards the hem of the garment. This has a slightly more slimming effect.

How to prepare and stitch a dart

1. Cut out garment and mark the dart on both layers of material, preferably using tailor tacking. Place one tailor tack exactly at the point of the dart.

2. Fold the fabric WS out and arrange so that the tailor tacks meet. You now have one row of tacks uppermost, running to the folded edge.

3. Put in a couple of pins, placing them across the dart, not along the line of tacks which is the temptation (a). Place a final pin ¼ in./6 mm beyond the last tack in order to hold it flat while you tack (b), otherwise the dart may move.

4. Tack the dart, starting at the raw edges and finishing off ¼ in./6 mm beyond the last tailor tack (where the pin is) (c). This is to prevent the machine from trampling the tacking ends into the fabric as you may damage the material as you dig to remove the thread. Press the folded edge lightly (d).

5. Machine, starting from raw edge and working to the point. Stop precisely at the final tailor tack and either reverse to fasten off or leave ends long enough to sew in (e).

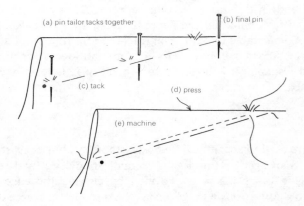

(a) pin tailor tacks together   (b) final pin
(c) tack   (d) press
(e) machine

It helps to lower the foot at an angle so that it is pointing towards the end of the dart; it is quite difficult to machine at an angle, especially after practising straight machining and edge-stitching.

6. Remove the tacking and also the tailor tacks. Both should come out easily but if you are left with a stubborn tailor tack use your eyebrow tweezers to pluck it out. Never use scissors for removing tacking, use a bone or plastic bodkin instead (see Equipment, page 13).

7. See that ends of machining are fastened off and trimmed close to the fabric.

Pressing a dart

Use your sleeve board or pressing pad, or, if you have neither, roll a towel into a pad. Place dart flat and still folded to begin with, and press the row of stitching. Open out the fabric WS upper-most and slide on to board or pad so that the dart is straight and the point is only $\frac{1}{4}$ in./6 mm from the edge of the pressing pad. This position ensures that you will not flatten the bulge that you have been at such pains to produce in the right place. Run the iron close to the stitching along both sides of the dart; it should now be standing upright.

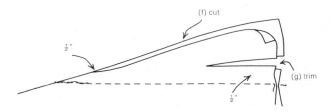

Note: Bulky fabrics: If it appears that the double layer will be too bulky (three layers if you count the garment), at this moment cut the dart along the fold to within $\frac{1}{2}$ in./13 mm of the point (f). Trim away surplus of dart to $\frac{1}{2}$ in./13 mm wide all the way along (g).

Press a folded dart to one side by running the iron along the side and gently knocking it over to one side, in the right direction remember. Press a cut dart as you would press an open seam, flattening the point.

Turn work to RS and press to remove creases and to check that the line of the dart is straight. Turn back again and press the WS firmly.

7. Tucks

These can also provide shaping if stitched for part of the way into a section of a garment. For example: from shoulder down to just above bust level (this makes the bust appear bigger, though) or from cuff up into a sleeve instead of gathers.

Tucks can also be purely decorative and in that case they are stitched for the whole length of that section of the garment, sometimes with rows of embroidery or ribbon in rows between the tucks.

If your pattern gives you a piece to cut out for tucking, cut it larger to allow for fraying and for the fact that you cannot really machine perfectly right at the raw edge, however careful you are. After working the tucks pin the paper pattern up, removing the tucks completely, lay it on the folded fabric, cut out and mark turnings.

How to prepare and stitch rows of tucks: Pleat-tucks

1. Cut out, making sure the grain is perfectly in position. Note that it is wise to practise on a small scrap of fabric first, trying out tucks with both the warp and the weft grain as some fabrics may pucker in one direction.

2. Run a row of small tacking stitching to mark the centre of the tuck (a) exactly on the straight grain starting with the tuck at the far left of the piece, RS towards you.

3. Fold fabric with tacking on edge and tack the desired width from the fold (b). The pattern will indicate how far this is. Use a marker to keep your tacking straight.

4. Press the fold.

5. Machine the tuck, stitching just to the inside of the tacking. i.e. making the tuck narrower by the width of the machine needle (c). This has the advantage of allowing the tacking stitches to be removed easily but also the tendency is to make tucks wider than they should be, partly due to the amount taken up at the folded edge, partly due to the thickness of the line on the pattern.

Pressing a pleat-tuck

Press in the same way as for a dart but work flat on a sleeve board or ironing board. Press the tuck to one side.

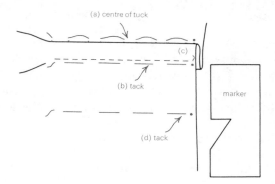

Making the rest of the tucks

1. Using your marker, adjust to the width shown on the pattern, to make another row of tacking parallel with the machining (d) (or the folded edge).

2. Fold on the tacking, tack, press, machine and press as for the first tuck.

Continue in this way until the whole area is covered. You can either press all tucks in one direction or you could press half the other way and decorate the centre, if it is the centre front, for instance with ribbon or buttons.

Machined tucks using special foot

Many machines include a tucking foot which will make rows of pin-tucks. Each tuck fits into a groove in the base of the foot while you work the next tuck so the foot automatically keeps them all straight. Follow the instructions in the machine handbook for type of needle, threading and use.

It will help to baste the fabric on to a backing such as cotton lawn, light-weight Vilene, or even tissue paper for fine fabrics (it will tear away afterwards).

Pressing

Press each tuck separately but do not press them to one side, they should stand upright.

8. Hand Sewing

The prospect of hand sewing horrifies anyone without experience, but with the right attitude of mind, and once you get the hang of it, it becomes one of the more relaxing parts of sewing and certainly the one which provides the most pleasure and enjoyment.

Make sure three things prevail before you consider a hand-sewing session:

1. See that you have plenty of time and are not going to have to hurry.

2. Make sure you are comfortable. An armchair provides handy pincushions.

3. Have everything for the job within easy reach, namely, thread, small 'between' needles, wax, small scissors, bodkin, for removing tacking. Later you will need the iron too.

When you must hand sew

Hand work must be done when you do not wish the stitching to show on the right side and also when it is more accurate to work from the right side, e.g. ends of waistbands (page 70), cuffs (pages 80–4).

Preparation

1. Take the end of thread from the reel, undo about 12 in./30·5 cm (the length from your wrist to your elbow), bite off the thread and keep the end in your mouth while you pick up the needle. Use a No. 6, 7, 8 or 9 Between, depending on the weight of fabric being used.

2. Hold needle in left hand (or right if you are left-handed), take thread from mouth and pass through eye of needle.

3. Take thread with thumb and forefinger of other hand and pull through.

How to make a knot

1. As your thumb and forefinger pull the thread through, wind thread once round forefinger (a).

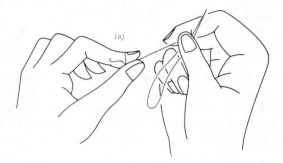

2. To make knot use thumb to slide off end of finger. Pull resulting knot right to end of thread.

If it doesn't work it simply means you didn't twist it enough times as you ran your thumb down your forefinger.

This is the correct size of knot for all work, anything larger will show, anything smaller will not hold the thread firmly.

When to use a knot

Practically always. It is the strongest way of starting a thread and less irritating than trying to use a back stitch.

Length of thread

For all permanent hand stitches use about 12 in./30·5 cm. If you are tacking, basting or tailor tacking (see pages 5 and 20) you can use a thread as long as from your shoulder to your wrist. This is because you will be making larger stitches and also there is a possibility that you will be standing up and therefore further away from the work.

Body position

Sit almost hunched over the work for all hand sewing with short thread. Position yourself comfortably and stitch. You will find that the short thread only allows the lower part of your arm to move: your upper arm, shoulder and head remain immobile and this enables you to make small, even stitches. A longer thread moves the whole body and you even lose focus on the work. This not only means it takes time to settle again to concentrate but you lose the rhythm of stitching. Only at the end of the thread should you move and sit up for a moment to re-thread the needle.

Tension

Much is written about tension in machining and knitting, but the same rules apply to hand sewing. You must pull the thread through at the same rate and to the same tightness with each stitch to achieve perfectly even stitches. This is easily done with the short thread and position described.

Hand position

The left hand (or right) holds the work flat with only the thumb on top (b). *Never* wrap it over the first two fingers as for embroidery. The right hand (or left) holds the Between needle, which is short, between the thumb and forefinger. The tailor's thimble is on the middle finger and the eye of the needle rests against the side of it (c).

To make a stitch insert the needle, pushing at the same time with the thimble, move the thumb and forefinger forward without losing touch with the thimble. Take hold of the point of the needle and pull through, again pushing with the thimble. In this way each stitch is made in one movement, pulling the thread right out to its furthest extent. After practice it becomes a quick circular movement rather than a series of separate stitches.

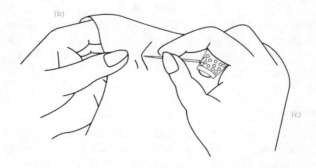

9. Pressing

Pressing is the single most important aspect of dressmaking because carried out correctly, it transforms a home-made garment into a well-finished one.

As with the other areas of dressmaking, it is an art only acquired with a great deal of practice. Different materials need different treatments with the iron and it is only by working on the fabric that you will discover the best way of dealing with it.

To be effective pressing has to be lasting, for instance, when pressing open a seam you should continue to press the turnings until they lie flat and stop springing up when you remove the iron. To obtain this lasting effect you need a combination of heat, pressure, moisture and, of course, the patience to wait while these three take effect.

Pressure

This is a combination of the weight of the iron and the amount of pressure you add by leaning on the iron. Again, try it out because some fabrics need a great deal more than others.

Heat

This varies according to the fibre content of the cloth you are pressing. It is best to try out the iron on a spare piece of fabric first.

Moisture

Few fabrics will take a permanent or professional looking press without the aid of moisture to persuade them to take up a new position. The amount of moisture needed varies with the fabric. On the whole, the thicker and more solid the fabric the more moisture is needed, but there are some, knits especially, that become soggy and stretched when too wet, so practise on a spare piece first. The moisture can be provided by a steam iron, although remember that the amount of steam is controlled and may be either too much for the fabric, or, more likely, too little. Moisture can also be provided by using a damp cloth either on its own with an ordinary iron or in conjunction with a steam iron. Use a piece of butter muslin, about ¾ yd/68 cm (or a baby's muslin napkin cut up), as a pressing

cloth. Muslin does not hold too much water so you are unlikely
to spoil light fabrics, yet you can fold it in half, or several times,
if you need more moisture.

When to press

It is vital to press properly every piece of machining that you do.
If you proceed to the next process you will find pleats and wrinkles
appearing and a generally amateurish finish will result. Once you
have passed a process you can never return to press it properly.
Keep the iron and board ready and usable every time you sew, so
that you can run the iron along every row of machining as you do
it to embed the thread into the fabric before proceeding to press the
process thoroughly into its final position.

How to press

Try not to slide the iron or its heel will cause wrinkling. Begin by using the toe of the iron to press stitching and then to press open the seam etc. After working with the toe, then use the iron flat, but use only the toe plus the first few inches of the iron base, not the heel. This involves holding the iron almost sideways, or at least at an angle, and this is the best position as you haven't too much of the work covered at a time.

If you are using a muslin cloth never drape it over the work but use only a small corner under the iron so that you can see what you are doing. Another advantage of muslin is that you can see through it.

When working on heavier fabrics, or putting in pleats or trouser creases, it will help to bang the steam into the fabric after removing the iron and the cloth. Use a proper pressing block or the back of a good heavy clothes brush (the bristle side can be used to brush up any flattened surface too), or even a book. Leave the block in position until the area is completely cold and then proceed to the next section.

Tailor's soap is useful for rubbing under obstinate turnings, the backs of pleats or the final press on trouser creases. If you cannot buy tailor's soap use a hard washing soap, dry.

Stretching or loss of shape

Ideally the material should be supported while you press. Heat and moisture soften fabric and if the weight of a garment is hanging below the board the garment can become stretched shapeless or fluted. The best arrangement is to use a sleeve board standing on an ironing board or table. This will also ensure that you press a small area at a time instead of trying to hurry. The table then supports the garment while you work.

Pressing shaped areas

Wherever you have shaping it is essential not to press the area flat again. Use the end of your sleeve board as a rounded shape and press darts, for instance, with the point exactly at that end. Alternatively make a small oval pressing pad, stuffed with cut-up nylons, and stand this on the sleeve board. Press gathers, too, by holding the gathers themselves just off the edge of the sleeve board and running the tip of the iron into them.

With bigger and more difficult areas of shaping, such as armholes and sleeve heads, roll up a hand towel into a pad and hold this in one hand, drape the garment over it and press with the iron in the other hand.

Note: Remember that pressing is a slow job and cannot be hurried. It is this and hand sewing that make dressmaking a craft which requires time and patience.

10. Fitting

There is no quick or easy way to learn fitting, nor is there a quick or easy way of doing it. It is a subject you learn about as you go along, gaining experience with each garment you make. Sometimes, if you have a particular figure problem, you find the same fault cropping up with each outfit, but often you will discover completely new problems to be conquered on each garment you make.

There is no substitute for fitting. All garments must be tried on before any machining is done and again at every stage of making, before stitching up, not afterwards when it is too late. Even if you are using the same pattern you must still try on because different fabrics behave in different ways.

There are three basic areas of adjustment no matter what the garment is, and they are:

Shape – for instance, darts.
Width – side seams.
Length – shoulder to waist, waist to hem.

As you begin to make things you will realize how vast the subject is, but here are a few problems that are always cropping up.

1. Problems of shape – Darts

Darts must always point in the direction of a bulge on the body, e.g. bust, bottom, elbow, shoulder blade.

Begin by checking that this is so (a); if not, undo the dart and repin in the correct direction (b).

The dart should not be too long or the garment will be tight.

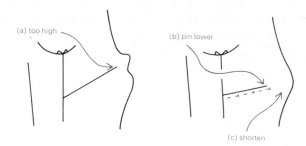

(a) too high   (b) pin lower   (c) shorten

Check that it finishes at least ¾ in./20 mm short of the bulge, or more for a looser fit (c). If the dart is too long or too short, undo tacking at point and repin to correct length.

The dart must also provide sufficient shaping for the bulge. If there seems to be a pocket of unfilled fabric unpick the dart or darts and repin making smaller at the base. If wrinkles of tightness appear round the area (d) undo the dart and repin making the base wider (e). This will often mean using up a little of the seam allowance at the nearest cut edge (f).

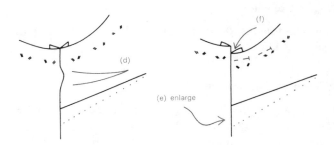

(d)   (f)   (e) enlarge

Gathers

Gathers also provide shaping and the same rules apply as for darts except that gathers are placed further than ¾ in./20 mm from the bulge concerned. Look at gathered sections and redistribute the fullness if necessary. If a whole area, e.g. skirt, appears too full, reduce the gathers and then cut the surplus fabric off the side edge.

2. Problems of width – Centre front or centre back seams

Look at these to see if there is surplus fabric at the neckline, chest, or shoulder blades and if so, pin out a small amount to correct (g). Do not overdo this alteration as it might prove best to take very little here and more from the side seams.

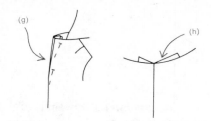

Side seams

If too loose, pin out surplus. If too tight, undo and repin. There is no need to take equal amounts from back and front. For example, if a bodice is loose only at the front on a broad-backed figure, then pin out fabric only on the front (h). Try to keep side seams hanging straight.

3. Problems of length

Beginners automatically worry about skirt lengths, but there are other areas to look at first.

Shoulder to base of armhole

If there seems surplus fabric here at front or back, undo seams and lift the shoulders until the fabric lies smoothly.

If the garment is dragging or lifting at this point then undo shoulders and release some of the seam allowance.

If the figure has rounded, square or sloping shoulders or a hollow chest you may not be taking an even amount off the back and the front. Nor may you be taking an equal turning all along the shoulder seam.

Base of armhole to waist

Next examine this area and adjust the waist seam accordingly. If you are making a one-piece dress, it is essential to check your back neck to waist measurement and, if necessary, to alter the pattern pieces before cutting out (see Checking and Altering the

Pattern, page 11). Small adjustments to this length can be made when fitting the shoulder seams, but this will mean re-marking the neckline and the armhole by laying the pattern to the new shoulder line. The bust shaping may also need adjusting.

Waist to hipline

Surplus fabric will appear as wrinkles across the body either at the front or, more usually, at the back below the waist (i). Once again undo the waist seam and pin out the surplus. You will find this gives you a more curved waist line (j). At the back the problem is caused by a hollow or sway back. At the front it is caused by a bulging tummy or high hip bones.

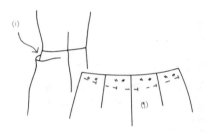

Hip to hem

This is where skirt length comes. It is often best to measure an existing skirt even if you then add a little to make it longer. Put on the garment and fasten it up and find someone to measure the hemline evenly from the floor. Wear the correct shoes and stand quite still in your normal posture. Your assistant should kneel on the floor with a long ruler (screw it to a block of wood to make it stable), or a hem marker, and work her way round pinning or chalking an even distance from the floor. Take the garment off and immediately turn up and tack on this line before the chalk rubs off or the pins fall out. Pin surplus hem fabric up and try on again before finishing hem as described on pages 47–51.

Rules for fitting

Remember the following rules when fitting:
1. Do it often.
2. Pin the alteration, tack it and try on again before machining.
3. Make a note on the pattern of what you had to alter.

Note: It helps, especially if you have to fit yourself, to put the garment on inside out for the first fitting, but do check the right way before stitching.

11. Hems

To make a hem you must turn up the raw edge of a garment. It can be a dress or skirt hem or the bottom of a jacket or trousers or the lower edge of a sleeve.

There are several methods to choose from depending on the effect you hope for. The following four methods are all easy enough for beginners to tackle but all should be worked with great care because a bad hem can spoil a garment completely.

Fullness in shaped hems

If you follow the methods described you will have little problem with fullness because with each type you will be tacking below the neatening, which is the fullest part. You can also slightly draw in fullness with your hand stitches, not by pulling the thread tight but by making tiny puckers of hem edge between the stitches.

However, the secret lies in avoiding the problem altogether. The more flared the edge, the greater the fullness and so the hem should be kept narrow.

Hem depth on a flared garment, whether it is a sleeve, jacket or skirt edge should be no more than $\frac{3}{4}$ in./6 mm and the fabric should be turned up only once, using either Method 1 or Method 3, to finish.

1. Hem turned up and hand finished

Suitable for all dresses, skirts, jackets, sleeves.

Advantages: Invisible. Helps garment to hang well.

(a) Mark hem line level (for dresses, skirts, etc., see Fitting, page 45). For sleeves, trousers, or jackets mark with chalk or tailor tacks on the right side. Check pairs of trousers legs and sleeves to see that they measure the same.

(b) Turn up on line (a) and tack ⅛ in. /3 mm from fold (b).

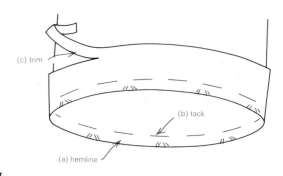

(c) trim

(b) tack

(a) hemline

Pressing

Place work on sleeve board, working in very short sections and turning the fabric, and press the *folded edge only*. Never let the iron stray on to the raw edge but press only the fold. Use a steam iron or a damp muslin cloth and dry iron and press firmly but not too heavily; this is not the final press.

(c) Trim raw edge down to re᷄ ᷄᷄red depth (c). The hem depth varies according to several points:

: if the edge is curved as, for instance, on a flared skirt, the depth of hem should be between ¾ in./2 cm and 1¼ in./3·2 cm.

: if the fabric is bulky the hem depth should be no more than 1¼ in./3·2 cm. or the garment will eventually sag.

: if the fabric is light-weight and fairly straight the hem depth can be up to 2 in./5 cm.

: on sleeves turn up between ½ in./13 mm and 1 in./2·5 cm.

: on trousers 1¼ in./3·2 cm.

When you progress to children's clothes you may want to break all these rules and allow good hems on everything.

(d) Neaten the raw edge with a small zigzag stitch (d) or, if fabric does not fray (e.g. jersey) with the blind hem stitch on the machine, or, by far the most satisfactory way is to finish by hand: work a row of straight machine stitching $\frac{1}{4}$ in./6 mm from the edge (or even do it before trimming down the raw edge). Trim away a few inches close to the machining, overcast from left to right, trim a little more and so on (see Seams, pages 25–7, for details). As you overcast pull the thread fairly tight as this will help to draw up any fullness.

(e) Tack neatened edge to garment (e).

(f) With fold of hem towards you (f) lift up the neatened edge and catch stitch $\frac{1}{4}$ in./6 mm under the edge, that is, immediately below the neatening (g).

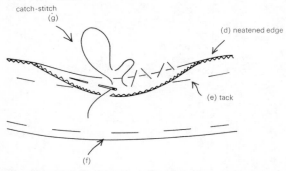

Work catch-stitch from right to left. Begin with a knot hidden in the hem section, use short pieces of thread and a No. 7 or 8 Between needle (see Hand Sewing, page 36). Take up one thread only on the garment (or less on thick weaves) then $\frac{1}{4}$ in./6 mm further on take a slightly bigger, firmer stitch in the hem, move on $\frac{1}{4}$ in./6 mm and pick up one thread, and so on. Fasten thread off firmly in the hem, not the garment.

Every 4 in./10 cm or so, leave a loop of thread about $\frac{1}{2}$ in./13 mm in length to take any stretching that might occur, especially in jersey fabrics. A loose stitch will prevent the hem-line showing after the garment has been worn for a while.

It is rarely that the stitches show, even with beginners, but it is the pressure of the raw edge and a tight stitch that makes the hemline visible.

Pressing

Remove all tacking before pressing and press the fold only again. Turn to the right side and press from the fold up to, but not over, the hem edge.

If you feel you haven't a sufficiently good result, turn the work to WS again, take a piece of spare fabric, fold it if it is thin, and lodge it against the hem edge. This brings the level up and will prevent the iron rocking on the hem edge. Press again *lightly* over the whole hem and spare fabric.

2. Hem turned up and finished by hand or machine

Suitable for all thin fabrics, especially those that fray badly; also use machine finish on casual garments such as nightwear, beachwear, and also on children's clothes.

Advantages: Controls fraying. Hand method almost invisible, although on transparent fabric the double edge would show, so use method 3 or 4 below.

(a) Mark hemline, turn up, tack.

(b) Mark the hem edge according to the depths described under the previous method No. 1, but do not trim.

(c) Turn in and tack.

Pressing

Press folded edge as described under Method 1, and press the other folded and tacked edge, but for the latter lift off it the garment. Do not press it against the garment.

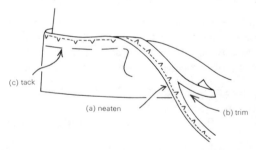

(d) There are three ways of treating this pressed edge: With a straight edge-stitch on the machine, with a small zigzag or blind stitch (a) or leave it as it is.

(e) Finally trim away the surplus raw edge on the WS close to the machining (b) or tacking.

Press again if machined.

(f) Tack hem flat to garment (c).

(g) Finish with slip hemming (d).

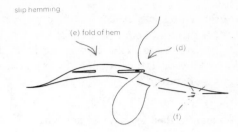

This is worked along the fold working towards you, or from right to left, whichever is more comfortable. Bury the knot in the fold and pick up one thread or less of the garment, move needle immediately into the fold and slide it through the fold for $\frac{1}{4}$ in./6 mm (e). Pick up one more thread, slide needle through fold and so on. Keep thread loose to avoid the hem showing. Nothing should show on the RS except perhaps a few dents in fine fabrics, and only tiny v's of thread should show on the WS (f).

Pressing

Press as for Method 1, avoiding the actual hem edge, removing all tacking first.

3. Hem turned up once and machined

Suitable for lightweight and medium weight fabrics where you don't mind machining showing. Do not use on skirt or dress hems.
Advantages: Not bulky. Useful as casing for elastic: Quicker than hand finished. Can be decorative (see Cuffs, page 85).

   (a) Zigzag raw edge to neaten (or hand overcast).
   (b) Turn up $\frac{5}{8}$ in./1·5 cm to WS, tack.
   (c) Machine from RS $\frac{1}{2}$ in./ 1·25 cm in from edge. Remove tacks.

Pressing

Press from fold up to machining with toe of iron.

4. Hem turned up and held with Wundaweb

The Wundaweb slightly stiffens the hem so this can be used anywhere where this may be an advantage. Use on jackets, trousers, sleeves.

Can be awkward to cope with a flared hem by this method. Always try it first in case the Wundaweb shows through. The hem must be 1¼ in./3·2 cm in depth to take it. Wundaweb can be cut in half but the half width will only hold light and medium-weight fabrics and the hem could only be ¾ in./20 mm deep.

Advantages: Quick. No sewing necessary on non-fraying fabrics. Keeps garments in shape, particularly trousers, as the additional slight stiffness holds the fabric firmly.

(a) Mark hemline.

(b) Turn up, tack and press fold (see Method 1, page 47, for details).

(c) Trim to exactly 1¼ in./3·2 cm.

(d) Neaten this edge if the fabric frays, by any method described under hem 1.

(e) Press neatened edge.

(f) Arrange work on sleeve board, supporting remainder of garment on table or ironing board. Slip the Wundaweb into the hem. Push it down as far as possible so that it does not show and does not quite reach the neatened edge (if it does the pressing will make the hem show).

Pressing

Press the hem in sections, up to the neatened edge, using steam iron or dry iron with damp muslin. Take care not to stretch the Wundaweb when placing it in position or the hem will contract.

Press each few inches of hem twice. Remove tacks, turn work to RS and press again lightly. Turn to WS and press again, building up the thickness as described in Method 1, page 49.

It is essential to press four times on Wundaweb, using moisture each time, otherwise neither heat nor moisture penetrates the cloth sufficiently to melt the Wundaweb and secure a permanent bond. When quite dry lift edge gently and inspect. If you can see white you must press again. If you can see only melted strands of adhesive then the hem will never come down.

This hem can be altered on some fabrics by pulling it gently away, but open weaves or fine fabrics will not stand the strain. If letting a hem down, re-stick with Wundaweb and brush off the old adhesive with a wire brush such as a teazle brush used for knitting.

12. Other Edge Finishes

On a curved edge it is often better not to attempt to turn up a hem but to choose another method of finishing the edge. None of the following three methods is difficult.

Method 1. Double fabric edge

Where to use: On any long curved edge such as the neck and front edges of a housecoat or wrap-over garment; sleeves or hems.

(a) Fold spare fabric at a right angle so that warp threads lie over weft threads (a). The fold you have is on the cross of the fabric and will stretch. If you have a cutting out board use the diagonal line on it as a guide. You can often cut quite long strips from spare fabric if you examine your left over pieces before folding.

(b) Cut along fold, holding with a few pins if fabric is springy (b).

(c) Measuring from raw edges cut strips 2 in./5 cm wide, cutting sufficient to finish the whole garment edge.

(d) Press strips, stretching slightly. Join together by placing end to end RS up with angled ends meeting (c) then flip over top one, keeping edges together. Stitch $\frac{1}{4}$ in./6 mm from edge, press joins open.

Beginners often find this confusing but two points may help: first remember that the join itself is on the straight grain, and secondly, back-stitch the joins by hand the first few times you join crossway strips (e).

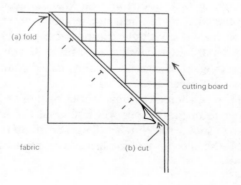

(a) fold

cutting board

fabric   (b) cut

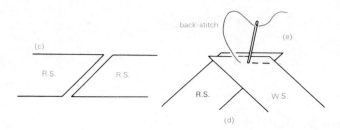

(e) Fold strip in half WS together to make a long folded strip.

(f) Place strip to RS garment edge but drawing strip back from edge slightly so that you take the usual $\frac{5}{8}$ in./15 mm turning off the garment but only $\frac{1}{4}$ in./6 mm off the strip. Tack. If strip goes right round edge you will first have to trim and join on the straight where the ends meet.

(g) Machine from strip side $\frac{1}{4}$ in./6 mm in from edge.

(h) Press row of machining. Trim edges down to $\frac{1}{4}$ in./6 mm with medium scissors. Neaten by zigzag or overcasting (f).

Pressing

Working on RS use toe of iron to press folded edge outwards but turnings underneath towards garment. Turn over and press WS (g). Turn back and press RS again.

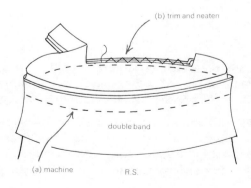

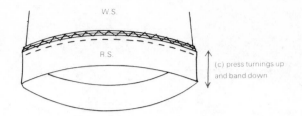

(c) press turnings up and band down

Method 2.   Double binding

This is similar to the double finish but is more difficult to manage and can be too bulky on any except medium and light fabrics. There is also the single bina method but this has not been included because it is more difficult still.

Where to use: Necklines, sleeves.

(a) Cut crossway strips as described above, join and press in the same way.

(b) Place on RS garment, once more taking ⅝ in./15 mm turning on garment but ¼ in./6 mm only on binding.

(c) Tack and machine (a).

(d) Trim all turnings to slightly less than ¼ in./6 mm (b).

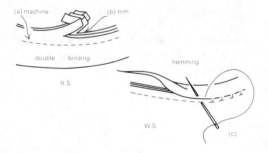

Pressing

Use toe of iron to press binding outwards on WS, on RS, work but turnings must also be pressed in the same direction. Turn to WS and check that all is flat by pressing again. Return to RS and press again.

(e) With WS work towards you, fold binding down on to machine stitches. Tack, taking care not to stretch binding and produce bubbles. In fact it helps to start in the middle and tack a few inches and then tack a few inches here and there before completing the gaps left.

(f) Hem into every machine stitch to finish (c).

Pressing

Press again lightly but do not squash the nice fat roll you have made.

Method 3.   Facings

This is the method most often used to finish a shaped raw edge because it is invisible. It involves using a piece of fabric with one edge cut exactly to the shape of the edge of the garment. The facing when finished should never be less than 2 in./5 cm wide. Where to use: Necklines, shaped hem edges, anywhere where the edge is shaped.

(a) Follow your pattern instructions for cutting but pin facing to garment RS together *before* joining the facings (a).

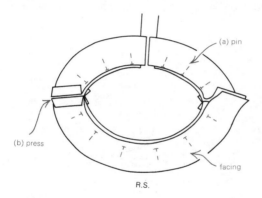

R.S.

This will be more accurate than joining first as edges stretch easily and also you may have made fitting adjustments.

(b) Press the facing turnings back so that the folds meet (b). Lift and join (by hand is easier to start with). Press open. Trim to ¼ in./6 mm. The illustration shows a neck facing but the method applies to any position.

(c) Tack all round on fitting line and machine. Press machining.

(d) Using medium scissors trim facing raw edge to ⅛ in./3 mm, trim garment raw edge to ¼ in./6 mm. Snip with small scissors towards machining every ½ in./13 mm at least to allow facing to lie flat (c).

(e) Roll facing to WS an inch at a time and tack a little below the fold. If you roll your facing fractionally to WS garment it will not show in wear (d). Press edge well.

(f) Baste remainder of facing to garment holding over hand to keep shape. Trim and neaten outer raw edge by machining or hand.

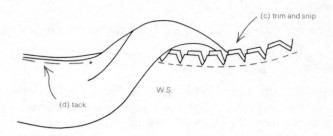

(g) Where facing crosses seam, e.g. shoulders, herringbone across raw edge (e).

(h) Finally hold remainder of facing down by slipping short strips of Wundaweb underneath and pressing well as described before. Try the Wundaweb on a scrap of fabric first to make sure it doesn't show.

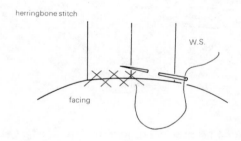

13. Fastenings

After making a series of tent-style gowns, Eastern djellabas and wrap-over blouses, skirts and housecoats there comes the moment when you must tackle something with fastenings. The following are all easy enough for beginners and you can substitute them for any of the more complicated fastenings that may be described in your pattern.

Only when you feel up to it should you progress to even the easy buttonholes (page 86) because they cannot be corrected, whereas all those described below can be unpicked and put right.

All fastenings need to be securely attached as they take a lot of strain. Many are best sewn on with buttonhole stitch (see page 62). This may seem unnecessarily laborious to you but it is well worth the extra effort.

1. Sewing on a button

Where to use: For holding tabs in position; for decoration, sewn right through instead of with a buttonhole; and in conjunction with some of the other fastenings that follow, also obviously for repairs.

Must be sewn to two layers of fabric plus interfacing if possible.

(a) Mark position with chalk cross.

(b) Thread needle with double thread, a fairly long piece, put à knot in the end.

(c) Wax the thread by running it through beeswax a couple of times, then holding the knot between thumb and forefinger let thread lie across palm and using other palm, twist the thread. Do this by rubbing one palm across the other. Wind the few inches that are twisted round the thumb, holding the knot, and continue until you reach the needle.

(d) Make a stitch on the chalk cross. Make two more stitches, stabbing right through all layers of fabric and passing needle up again each time.

(e) Cut off the knot.

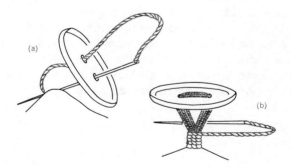

(f) Slide button on to needle and sew on taking needle into and out of fabric in one movement (a). Next pass needle up through hole in button, then once more pass needle through button and in and out of fabric in one movement. It is vital for button to stand away from fabric so with each stitch lift the button to be sure there is a shank. This method of sewing is a great help in forming a shank.

Length of shank must equal total thickness of piece to be passed over the button, so it varies. It is not advisable to use a matchstick or other aid because that produces a shank of only one length.

(g) Work plenty of stitches but not so many that centre of button looks bulky.

(h) Finish with needle and thread between fabric and button and wind thread round shank, starting from base and working to button, then winding down again (b).

(i) Pass needle several times through fabric at base of shank, pass needle to WS work and fasten off.

Direction of holes in button:

Two-hole buttons are sewn so that holes are horizontal along buttonhole, so they could be either vertical or horizontal. In all other positions the holes are horizontal with the strain, e.g. cuffs, collars, other neck fastenings, waists.

Four-hole buttons are sewn with one pair of holes in the horizontal position, like a cross, not a kiss.

2. Button and worked loop

Where to use: This is often used at an edge-to-edge opening, but can also be used where there is an overlap, e.g. cuffs. The only slight disadvantage is that the buttons can move within the loops, but it is a very easy fastening to work.

Sew buttons in position first.

(a) Wax a double thread and knot the end.

(b) Take a stitch on the edge of the garment, and run the needle through edge for $\frac{1}{4}$–$\frac{1}{2}$ in./6–13 mm depending on size of button.

(c) Take another stitch over the first, leaving a loop long enough for the button to slip through (a). Make it a tight fit as loops tend to stretch. Form about four or five loops together.

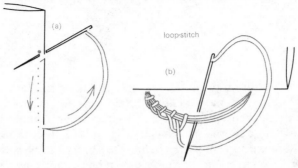

(d) Cut off knot.

(e) With needle at left and loop hanging towards you, work loop-stitches close together all round to form a good strong wire to fasten over buttons (b).

(f) Fasten off by running thread through fold of garment. Don't be tempted to run through to the next loop as the thread is now too weak, and anyway, if one loop breaks in wear they will all come undone.

3. Purchased frogs, chains etc.

Where to use: These fastenings are a boon to the newcomer to sewing because she can add a professional touch. Use on any overlapped opening where the additional decoration looks suitable. Never use too many as they are bulky; only, say, two or three.

(a) Place frog or chain on garment still fastened. Mark position with chalk or pin.

(b) Unfasten. Pin in position, or tack if bulky. With chains you will have to hold them in place. With frogs you can pin from WS.

(c) Stitch on strongly. If using a chain loop use buttonhole stitch (see Hooks, page 61) to hold some parts and oversew others, much depends on the design. Frogs are more easily attached with a very strong back-stitch from WS and then sewn again just under edge of cord from RS.

An alternative method on thick fabric is to work from WS and stitch on firmly using a half-back stitch.

The essential thing is to sew on as strongly as possible with a lot of stitches that are invisible to the onlooker. Also, if they tend to move, sew a press stud between (see below).

4. Velcro fastener

This is the specially produced nylon tape that cleverly fastens by simply pressing the two halves, looped and hooked, together.

Where to use: In place of almost any fastening on overlapping or edge-to-edge openings. It is slightly more bulky than some other fasteners but, depending on the position and the fabric, it can be used on cuffs, belts, waistbands, tabs, wrap-overs for fastening collars edge-to-edge or overlapped, and in place of buttonholes. In the last case use short pieces of Velcro rather than a long run. It is also a useful safety device against thieves on pockets, purses and handbags. In addition it is the best way of fastening detachable items such as frills, collars, cuffs, jabots, etc. You will soon think of plenty of ideas.

(a) Work out which piece of Velcro will be best facing the body, e.g. with trousers that will slip up over tights it will be best not to have the harsh hook side facing the body where it can catch on clothes.

(b) Cut off the length of Velcro required. I would recommend 3 in./7·5 cm for a waist or bikini fastening, or anywhere where the body expands, but at wrists you can use one piece vertically down the cuff and so use the width of it, which is either $\frac{7}{8}$ in./2·2 cm or $\frac{5}{8}$ in./15 mm. On a collar too there is no strain so use a narrow piece.

(c) Trim $\frac{1}{8}$ in./3 mm off the rough hook side. This makes sure it is well covered by the soft side.

(d) Sew in position with small hemming stitches, a fairly fine needle, No. 6 or No. 7, and single waxed thread, synthetic thread such as Coats 'Drima', not twisted. Sew all round. The cut edges will not fray.

An alternative method if it will not show on RS garment is to use a very small zigzag stitch on the machine.

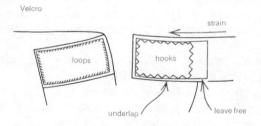

Tip

When sewing Velcro to waists or anywhere where there is a lot of body movement, do not sew quite to the end of the under piece. This will eliminate crackling and give a little ease.

5. Press studs

These come in a variety of sizes. Choose the smallest for fine fabrics and medium for medium fabrics. Big press studs do not hold any better than small ones. Always sew through a layer of fabric and a layer of interfacing if possible.

Where to use: Wrist openings, necklines, perhaps at waistline between buttons, but nowhere where there will be body strain or a tight fit. 'Knob' section always goes to outer part of garment.

Thicker 'well' section goes underneath.

(a) Mark exact position of knob sections with pin or chalk.

(b) Thread needle and wax thread (single) but do not twist. Knot the end.

(c) Take two deep small stitches in marked position. Cut off knot. Remove marking pin.

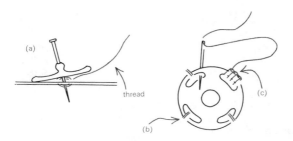

(d) Slip another pin through press stud and spear into position (a). Work one oversewing stitch in each of the four holes (b).

(e) Work small close buttonholes stitches to fill each hole passing needle below work from hole to hole. It normally takes four or five stitches (c) (see hooks).

(f) Pass needle to WS and fasten off firmly.

(g) Pin up opening. Pass pin through hole of knob and hole of well and push through the under layer. Mark the spot with another pin and start the thread as described for the knob section.

(h) Sew on this section in the same way using a pin first to position it, then a stitch in each hole, then buttonholing.

6. Hooks and eyes or bars

Choose the size in the same way as for press studs. Use bars rather than eyes as they take up less space, do not show, and give a steadier fastening.

Where to use: Anywhere where a press stud would be too weak.

(a) Mark position of hook, which should always be at least $\frac{1}{8}$ in./3 mm back from the edge.

(b) Use single waxed thread and start by anchoring the hook itself with 6 or 7 strong stitches passing through the fabric (though not to RS) and under the hook.

(c) Pass needle under to loop and work close buttonhole stitch round each loop (a).

buttonhole stitch

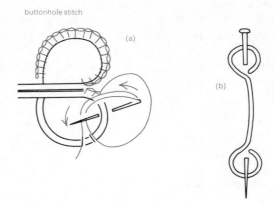

(d) Fasten off on WS.

(e) Fasten hook to bar, position bar by placing pin through both holes (b). Work close buttonhole stitch round both holes. If sewing on an eye the procedure is the same.

7. Rouleau bow

You can replace any edge-to-edge fastening with a rouleau bow. Where to use: Necklines, wrists. It is easiest to use where you can bind the edge at the same time (see Designing for Beginners, page 92).

(a) Cut a length of crossway strip, joining if necessary as described under Edge Finishes, page 52.

(b) Fold in half and press, stretching slightly.

(c) Place crossway strip to RS garment, taking usual $\frac{5}{8}$ in./15 mm of garment, but $\frac{1}{4}$ in./6 mm of binding.

(d) Pin each end of binding to wrist, leaving enough at each end to tie bow, but also making sure wrist is correct size.

(e) Ease up gathers, pin, tack, machine.

(f) Remove tacks. Trim edges to less than $\frac{1}{4}$ in./6 mm using medium scissors.

(g) Fold binding over to WS and tack down on to gathers. Finish ends by folding raw edges in and bringing to meet folded edge. Tack and press. Slip-stitch tie ends and hem into machining along gathered section.

(h) Finish ends by tucking $\frac{1}{4}$ in./6 mm of raw edge inside tube with a pin.

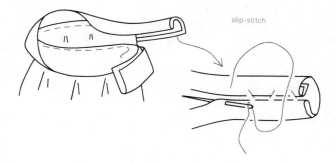

slip-stitch

8. Rouleau loop

This is a loop made from a crossway strip to fasten round a button. Cannot be used if there is no seam at edge of garment.

Where to use: In place of a thread loop. They look attractive used with covered dome buttons.

(a) Cut and prepare a crossway strip but it should be only 1 in./ 2·5 cm wide. Fold in half with *right sides together* this time.

(b) Machine down centre of strip using synthetic thread which is strong and a very slight zigzag stitch if you can (a).

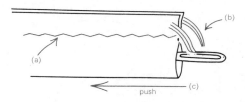

push

(c) Take a metal bodkin or elastic threader and slip into the end of tube. Sew eye of bodkin firmly to turnings (b). Push bodkin gently through to other end (c) and rouleau will pull through RS out.

(d) Form into loop to fit tightly over button, allow turnings, and put into seam. The distance between the two ends at the base will be between $\frac{1}{4}$ in./6 mm and $\frac{3}{4}$ in./20 mm depending on size of button. Machine in place first, then sew complete seam. Turn to RS and loop will appear.

9. Edge-to-edge fastening

It may not be advisable to have bulky fabric overlapping and fastening, but a neat edge-to-edge finish can be made by using Velcro.

Where to use: Fastening a collar at CB.

(a) After completing a collar, cut a piece of Velcro slightly shorter than the depth of the collar. Cut Velcro in half lengthwise to make it narrower.

(b) Sew the hooked side of the Velcro so that it extends beyond the collar but tuck it under the edge by $\frac{1}{8}$ in./3 mm and hem firmly (a).

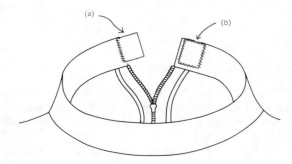

(c) Sew the loop side of Velcro to the other edge of the collar but place it completely under the collar and hem in place. When the Velcro is fastened the collar is edge-to-edge (b).

14. Zip Fasteners

The zip is probably the fastener in most common use, but it presents a problem to dressmakers. The main reason for the problem is that the zip tape is usually a closely woven, tough fabric which has to be stitched to the garment. The effect of the pressure of stitching through layers of sometimes quite thin material can cause wrinkling. Best results are usually obtained by stitching by hand.

The two methods described are the most foolproof for the inexperienced.

Concealed zip

These are special zips with the teeth attached to the edge of the tape so that when it is fastened the teeth roll back out of sight.

The main advantage to the beginner is that no stitching shows on the RS garment so she doesn't have to be nervous about keeping straight.

You may find that the instructions in the packet direct you to insert the zip before stitching the seam, but this makes fitting impossible at the correct stage so this is the method of insertion that I have worked out.

1. Stitch the seam and fasten stitching, leaving an opening $\frac{1}{2}$ in./10 mm shorter than the length of the zip teeth.

2. Stitch up the gap where the zip is to go; do this by machine, using a big stitch (a).

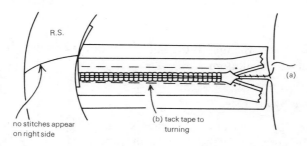

no stitches appear on right side

(b) tack tape to turning

3. Press open well.

4. With WS seam uppermost place zip, closed, RS down with teeth falling centrally over the seam. The zip tab should fall $\frac{1}{8}$ in./3 mm to $\frac{1}{4}$ in./6 mm below the fitting line at the top to allow room for the top to turn over or have the facing attached.

If you have difficulty in holding the zip in position use a pin at the top but never completely pin any zip into a seam or it makes the zip 'snake'.

5. Tack tape to seam turning only. Tack as close as you can to the teeth, but keep checking to make sure that the teeth are centrally over the seam join. Tack both sides (b).

6. Remove the machine stitches holding that section of the seam together. Open the zip.

Stitching by hand

Start at the top, roll the teeth over so that the stitches can be made really close to the teeth (c) and work half back stitch through tape and turning (d). Using double thread, waxed (page 57), work as far as the slider then move the slider up a little way (e) and

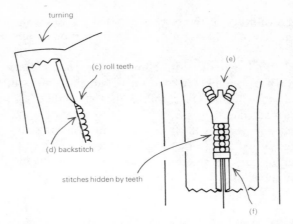

continue back stitching to the bottom. Work both sides (f). Do not stitch across the bottom.

Stitching by machine

Put the zipper foot on the machine and adjust or attach the special foot for concealed zips, such as the one produced by Lightning Fasteners. Stitch from top to bottom, stopping when you reach the slider. Move slider and stitch the last few inches of zip. Work both sides in the same way. Fasten off ends of thread well.

Remove all tacks and run zip gently up and down to roll teeth into position.

Never press after inserting.

Conventional zip – Even hems method

Turn in $\frac{5}{8}$ in./15 mm on each side of opening and tack near to fold (a).

Press, taking care not to stretch the edge.

Place the zip in position so that one folded edge extends slightly more than halfway over the teeth. The tab should lie slightly below the fitting line.

Tack through fabric and zip tape, working from the top of the zip to the bottom (b). Repeat on second side and then join the two folded edges (which will slightly overlap) together with an over-sewing stitch to prevent them being drawn apart by the final stitching (c). This is particularly likely to happen if you are going to sew in the zip by machine.

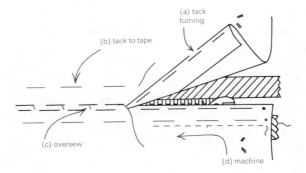

(a) tack turning

(b) tack to tape

(c) oversew

(d) machine

Machine or hand stitch from the RS so that the stitches will lie down the centre of the zip tape (d). The best result is obtained by stitching from top to bottom on both sides, but not stitching across the bottom as this can cause a bubble in the fabric.

Use stab stitch (see page 88) if sewing by hand. Use a zipper foot if sewing by machine.

15. Waistbands

These must be well strengthened to withstand the strain of wear and they must be long enough to circle your waist and overlap.

Suggested stiffening:

Pelmet Vilene (stiff)

Petersham (softer)

Firm iron-on Vilene (softer still)

The best way to ensure a fit is to make the band fit you. Your pattern will provide a waistband but it may not be exactly your size if you have altered the waist at fitting. Also if you add a length of fabric to a waistline, making the band fit the top of the skirt, in most cases it will not fit you.

Making a waist-fitting aid

Take a piece of petersham and put it round your waist; trim it until it overlaps by 3 in./7·5 cm. Sew 3 in./7·5 cm of Velcro to the ends (a). Do this roughly by machine so that you will never be

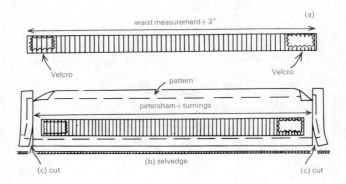

tempted to use this petersham in a skirt – it is far too useful as a fitting aid. Do make sure that it fits you snugly. If you put on weight, or even lose it, you can lap the Velcro over more, or less, and make a pencil mark where your new waist is.

Cutting and interfacing the band

1. Place pattern on fabric, using the selvedge direction if you can as it is stronger (b). Lay the petersham on top and cut to the width of the pattern, but to the length of the petersham *plus end turnings* (c). Mark the middle of the band for the whole of its length with chalk on RS.

2. Place pattern on interfacing ready to cut to length, but if using either Pelmet Vilene or petersham, fold back the pattern turnings and half the width of the band first and cut the interfacing exactly the width the band will be when finished. If using the lighter method it can be included in the whole band. Cut interfacing. Place in position on band.

3. There are three main methods of attaching the interfacing.

(a) By pressing, but only if using iron-on interfacing.

(b) By machining with a straight or zigzag stitch (d). This applies to both stiffer varieties. It should be tacked on first. The machining will, of course, show on the RS when finished.

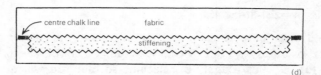

(c) By slipping Wundaweb between the fabric and the inter-facing and pressing well to hold.

Attach interfacing by one of these methods. Press.

4. It looks more attractive to have an *underlap* from the back than an overlap from the front which will be visible to people behind you, so place band to skirt, RS together, with 3 in./7·5 cm extending from back (e). Just the turning should extend from the front (f).

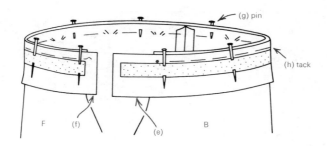

5. Pin band to waist, placing pins vertically (g). The interfacing should be where you are pinning. Match band to the skirt fitting line.

6. Tack just off the edge of the interfacing in the case of the stiffer ones (h). Tack accurately, as the band tends to move under the machine.

7. Machine from waistband side right round and fasten off both ends securely. Remove tacks. Press row of stitching.

8. Trim raw edges down unevenly to about $\frac{1}{4}$ in./6 mm and a little more. Lift band and place on sleeve board with both turnings going up into band. Press on RS with toe of iron a few inches at a time (i). Press again on WS.

9. Turn in ends of band and tack (j). Fold band along chalk lines. Tack and press.

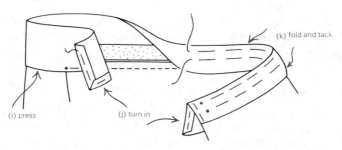

10. Tack again about $\frac{1}{2}$ in./13 mm below this through all layers of band (k).

11. Tack ends of band together. Work along length of band turning raw edge under. On the garment the fold should just allow the machine stitches to show. On the ends and overlap the folded edges should meet exactly.

12. Finish by slip-stitching ends and overlap (l) and along remainder hem into machining (m).

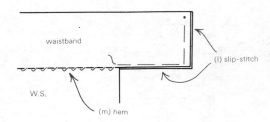

Pressing

Remove all tacks and press well on both sides.

16. Setting in Sleeves

This process shares a reputation with buttonholes as being the most daunting action in dressmaking.

As with everything, I break it down into simple stages to be tackled one at a time.

Complete the garment as far as you can, including finishing cuffs and sleeve edges and even the dress hem and fastenings as well if you like.

Getting the right sleeve into the right armhole

1. Lay the bodice on the table. You will see that the front of the armhole is more scooped out than the back.

2. Fold both sleeves along the seam and lay them down. You

will find that one edge is slightly more scooped than the other. This is the front of the sleeve.

3. Place each sleeve to its armhole, scooped edges together and put a pin to hold the sleeve to that side of the bodice.

Set in the underarm section

1. Lift bodice and arrange armhole in front of you with underarm seam in the centre.

2. Unpin sleeve and place sleeve seam to this underarm seam. Note that you are working with RS out on both sleeve and bodice (a).

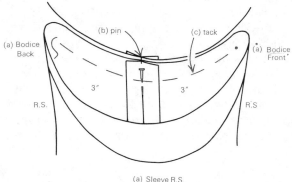

3. Pin the seams together and then pin a few inches of the under-arm seam (b). Both edges are roughly the same shape so it isn't too difficult. Pin for about 3 in./7·5 cm on each side of the central pin, just until the sleeve head begins to change shape.

4. Tack this underarm section and fasten off tacking (c).

5. Pin and tack second sleeve in the same way.

Dealing with sleeve head

This is the worst area because the two edges are totally different in shape and also the sleeve head is slightly larger than the armhole. However, this second point provides a clue as to how to hold it. Whenever one edge is longer or more shaped than the other (as with a curved seam, which is really all a sleeve head is), place the longer or more shaped edge on top so that you can see how you are coping with the excess material. If you stuff the sleeve inside the armhole it will have to wrinkle up and you can only end up with a wrinkled sleeve head.

Having tacked the underarm, now pull the bodice over the sleeve head so that the bodice is inside out and the sleeve head is indeed wrinkled up. Take the armhole and sleeve head in your fingers and roll them back so that the sleeve head is now on top. You will immediately see that the sleeve head is no longer the problem that it was when it was within the armhole.

Pinning and tacking the sleeve head

1. Ease the centre of the sleeve head back to meet the shoulder seam of the bodice. You may have transferred the dot on the pattern at that point, but it doesn't matter too much if you haven't because you can see the centre as it is flat for about 2 in./5 cm. In addition to this you will be trying on the sleeve, after which it may need altering anyway.

2. Place one pin at this point, across the seam line, picking up only a very small amount of fabric on the pin.

3. Spread your fingers out under the whole area and begin to pin the remainder, dividing and subdividing each half of the sleeve head, inserting more and more pins to break down the excess fullness into such small bumps that none will form a pleat when stitched (d).

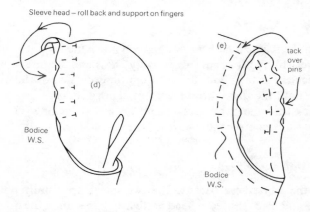

Sleeve head – roll back and support on fingers

(d)

Bodice W.S.

(e)

tack over pins

Bodice W.S.

4. You will probably have to move the pins several times before you are satisfied that the fullness is satisfactorily disposed of. A general rule is that there will be slightly more towards the front of the sleeve where the shoulder bone protrudes than at the back where the body hollows slightly.

5. Tack with small stitches over the pins. You may like to tack from the bodice side at this stage to ensure a good armhole line (e).

Stitching in the sleeve

1. Thread a needle with double sewing thread, waxed (see page 57 for waxing thread), work from sleeve side and stitch sleeve in using a half back stitch.

2. Work carefully over the areas of fullness, making sure no pleats appear. Remove tacking.

If you are new to hand sewing and cannot face all this, at least back stitch the sleeve head to control the fullness and then put work under machine and stitch right round armhole, from the sleeve side.

Pressing

Use a pad or rolled up towel, push it into the armhole under the sleeve head and press the join with the toe of the iron. Use a steam iron or a dry iron and damp muslin cloth. Both turnings should be pressed into the sleeve to support the sleeve head.

Do not press the underarm except to press the actual stitching, the sleeve and bodice should hang down together under the arm.

17. Collars

The usual method of attaching a collar is to machine it up first and then fit it to the neckline. I find it particularly difficult to obtain an accurate result this way so I work the stages of a collar in a different order. Try this method.

General rule

Insert zip, if any. Set one layer of the collar to the neck edge of the garment first. This join is, after all, an important one as it affects the set of the collar and on some styles the neck seam is visible. This method also does away with facing on most styles, which reduces bulk.

Order of construction

1. Insert the zip then cut out the collar. If you have altered the neckline or raised the shoulders remember to adjust the length of the collar accordingly by splitting in the middle and opening or by pleating out if there is surplus length.

2. Attach interfacing. See styles below for details of where to include it.

3. Pin neck edge of one layer of collar to neck edge of garment, snipping both edges, if necessary, to help in joining. Tack from collar side. Machine from end to end from the garment side following seam line.

4. Remove tacks. Snip turnings well every $\frac{1}{4}$ in./6 mm (a).

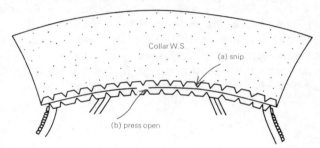

Pressing

This is a curved seam and it must remain so. Press open (b) a few inches at a time using the toe of the iron. Put the sections of seam over the sleeve board or over a pad or rolled-up towel. Turn work to RS and press again making sure you have a really good seam. Turn back to WS and press again. If any part is particularly stubborn on a springy fabric, slip very tiny pieces of Wundaweb under that part of the turnings.

Different collar styles

1. Shaped band collar (see Designing, page 94)

This is usually found on a high round neck but can be set a little lower. The collar normally fastens at CB above the zip. Cut two shaped pieces from pattern.

Order of Work.

(a) Interface WS of one piece of the collar with sew-in or iron-on Vilene which can be fairly crisp according to the fabric.

(b) Attach neck edge of collar to neck edge of garment. If there is an extension for fastening the collar allow this to extend at CB; the left side is best, so that it forms an underlap.

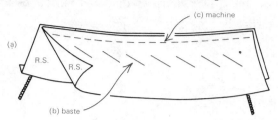

(c) Place second piece of collar RS against RS (a) of attached piece. Baste down centre (b) then tack along top edge.

(d) Machine top edge from end to end (c). Remove tacks. Snip and layer the turnings.

Pressing

Press as for neck join, over a pad.

(e) With WS garment towards you roll collar piece over so that the join slightly shows (d). Tack, not from end to end, but leaving about 2 in./5 cm free (e) at each end. Press edge.

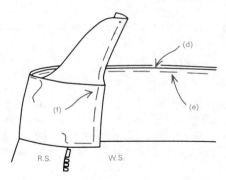

(f) Turn work so that RS garment is towards you, turn in and tack collar ends and lower edge of extension if any (f). Press.

(g) Bring collar ends together and tack. Slip stitch ends and extension.

To finish

Light fabrics: With both neck turnings up into collar, fold under raw edge of collar, tack down so that fold falls at centre of neck seam (g). Hem (h). Press. Remove tacks.

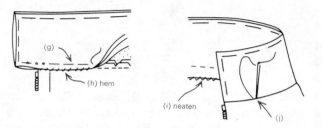

Medium and heavier fabrics: Tack raw edge flat, snipping if necessary. Neaten edge with overcasting (i) Then finish by stab stitching (page 88) through the join (j). Work from RS collar to make sure stitches sink invisibly into the seam. If there is an end extension slip stitch as usual but snip the turning $\frac{1}{4}$ in./6 mm in to allow the edge to lie flat.

Pressing

Press from WS first then turn and press RS well, keeping collar curved over sleeve board, pad or towel.

2. Soft tie collar (see Designing, page 93)

Often on blouses or soft-styled dresses. Only use light fabric that ties and drapes well. The pattern piece is cut on the straight with extensions allowed for tying. It is necessary to have a gap at CF but this can be worked by turning the seam allowance on to WS. Zip will be at CB. Cut two collar pieces.

Order of work

(a) Place collar pieces to neckline with the end turnings extending at CB (a) and pin to neckline with ties meeting at CF (b). Make a chalk mark on collar 1 in./2·5 cm on each side of CF (c). Unpin the pieces.

(b) Cut a strip of soft iron-on Vilene half the width of the collar

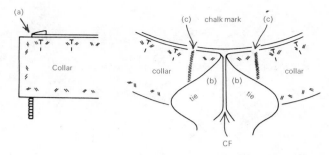

and interface from chalk mark to CB on each piece, against the neck edge.

(c) Tack and machine neck edge of collar pieces to neckline of garment, finishing machining at chalk mark, so leaving a 2 in./5 cm gap at CF. Snip and press neck join as before.

(d) Snip neckline turning at gap (d) and tack down to WS (e). This section may need snipping a couple of times. Neaten raw edge with overcasting (f) hold down by slipping a few pieces of Wunda-web underneath. Press.

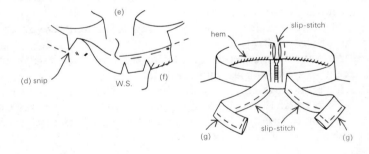

(e) Press remainder of neck turnings up towards collar. Turn in collar ends and tack. Turn under raw edges so that fold lies on machine stitching.

(f) Turn in all raw edges of tie ends of collar. Press. Tack folded edges together (g). Slip-stitch (see page 70) folded edges of ties together and ends of the collar at CB. Hem remainder of collar into machine stitches (see page 70) along neck edge.

(g) To fasten collar at CB (see Fastenings, page 64).

3. Shirt collar

This style is usually combined with a centre front opening either

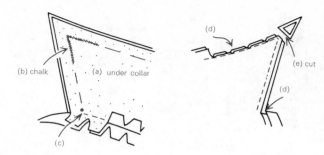

buttoned or zipped and details for that part can be followed from the instruction sheet with the pattern. The collar pattern can be straight or slightly shaped and is usually cut on the straight grain. Cut two collar pieces.

Order of work.

(a) Interface under collar with soft or medium sew-in Vilene.

(b) Attach neck edge of under collar to neck edge of garment. If the style has a front fastening remember to stitch collar to CF point only. Press join open as before.

(c) Place top collar section to under collar, RS together. Baste along centre. Tack round edge (a).

(d) Use ruler and chalk, or pencil, to draw collar points accurately. Do this on *under* collar (b).

(e) Machine from under-collar side, lowering needle precisely into the point where neck machining ends (c).

(f) Layer turnings, snip (d). Cut off corners close to machining (e).

(g) Turn collar through, rolling edges with fingers. Push bodkin up into point to ease out, but do not push too hard, then ease gently out with a pin from RS.

Pressing

Remove all tacks. Press collar edges from under side, press neck join from both sides. Press whole collar and rever from both sides, very carefully.

After pressing all collars

Put garment on hanger, roll collar into correct position and allow to cool before proceeding to next process.

(h) Push a small piece of Wundaweb up into the collar points, using your bodkin.

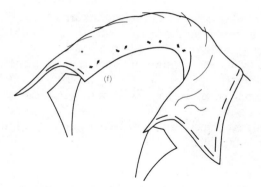

(i) With under collar towards you, roll edge and tack so that join just shows. Press edge.

(j) Fold collar into the position it will take up in wear and, still holding it in this position, baste along the curve where it folds (f).

To finish

Light fabrics: Turn under raw edge across back of neck from shoulder seam to shoulder seam. Snip turning at shoulder seam. Tack.

Medium and heavier fabrics

Tack raw edge flat, neaten with overcasting.

Completing rever section

(This can, of course, be an open rever or the style that buttons to the neck). If there is a separate front facing attach it to CF edge now.

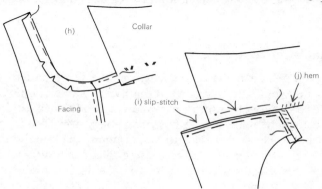

(a) From end of collar to CF extension turn in raw edge and tack. Also, turn in raw edge along neck edge of facing (h). Press with toe of iron.

(b) Fold facing into position so that raw edges meet along CF extension. Tack.

(c) From that point to shoulder seam turn in collar edge and tack down to neck join.

(d) Finally tack neck section of facing so that the fold meets the folded edge of the collar.

To finish

Press all tacked and folded edges with toe of iron. Slip stitch (page 70) folded edges together at CF corners and section from there to shoulder seam (i). Hem (j) (page 70) or stab-stitch (page 88) across back of neck. Hem edge of facing to shoulder turnings.

18. Cuffs

Cuffs are an attractive, always fashionable, way of finishing the wrist of a long sleeve. The traditional method requires an opening to be made in the sleeve by means of a slash which has to be neatened. This is too difficult for a beginner and here I give two methods which avoid it.

If you wish to avoid a cuff altogether see Designing for Beginners, page 92.

Preparation of sleeve and cuff

(a) You will have altered the length of the sleeve pattern as instructed on your pattern so cut out the sleeves. Cut on fabric folded double to be sure of cutting a pair and not two left ones, or, if you must cut singly, remember to turn the pattern over for the second sleeve and to check that the pattern is running the same way.

(b) The lower edge of a gathered sleeve will often be very unevenly shaped. The section which dips a little should come at the back of the arm, in line with the elbow and little finger (this gives the

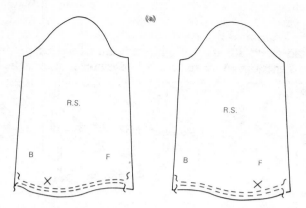

ease the elbow needs for bending). This is also usually where the opening is, if any, so that it is not visible to anyone looking at you from the front. Mark the position of the opening with a chalk cross on the RS.

(c) Insert the gathering threads omitting the sleeve turnings (a).

(d) Fold cuff pattern and put round wrist. It should overlap by $1\frac{1}{4}$ in./3·2 cm. Do not cut cuffs too long – all wrists vary in size.

(e) Cut cuffs, in line with the selvedge if possible. Try on again for size.

1. Sleeve with wrap-over cuff

Suitable for medium- to light-weight fabrics.

The cuff

Requirements: Medium or firm iron-on Vilene, about 4 in./10 cm Velcro *or* 2 in./5 cm if you like to cut it in half lengthwise. 4 buttons (optional).

Method

(a) Press interfacing to WS cuff. Mark turnings on RS with chalk or tracing wheel and carbon paper. Also chalk down centre of cuff.

(b) Pin cuff ends to sleeve edge, matching raw edges and with RS together. Keep the cuff inside and sleeve outside so that you can see gathers.

(c) Pull up gathers to fit. Tack. Machine from gathered side. Remove gathers.

(d) Press turnings up into cuff (b).

(e) Fold sleeve RS together, pin cuff ends together putting one pin across the join to make sure the edges meet accurately.

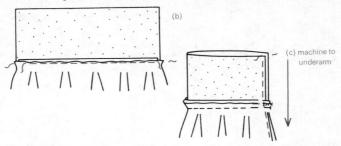

(f) Machine from cuff over the pin, stitching slowly, then machine to underarm (c).

(g) Press this seam open for the whole of its length. Trim turnings to $\frac{1}{4}$ in./6 mm within cuff.

(h) Fold cuff on chalk line and tack (d).

(i) Turn under raw edge of cuff on to machine stitching. Hem into machine (e).

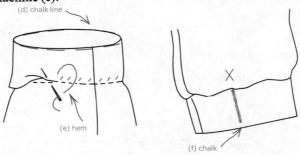

(j) On RS make a chalk mark on cuff in line with the X on the sleeve (f).

(k) Slip sleeve on arm and fold over cuff to fit wrist (g) matching edge of pleat to chalk line. Do not fit this cuff too tightly. Establish fold of pleat with a pin. Remove sleeve.

(l) Hem two pieces of Velcro in position so that when pressed together cuff fits wrist (h). The distance between the two pieces of Velcro will vary according to length of cuff and size of wrist.

(m) Fasten and fold wrap in correct direction. You can sew on two buttons if you like, on the outside (i).

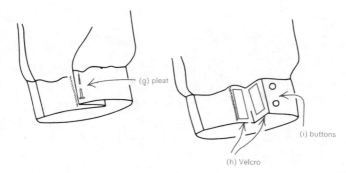

(g) pleat

(i) buttons

(h) Velcro

2. Sleeve with opening in seam

Requirements: Medium or firm iron-on Vilene, about 4 in./10 cm.
Velcro *or* 4 press studs.
4 buttons (optional).
About 3 in./7·5 cm Wundaweb.

Method

(a) Press interfacing to WS cuff. Mark turnings and centre of cuff, also mark 1¼ in./3·2 cm for underlap.

(b) On underarm sleeve seam make chalk mark 3 in./7·5 cm up from lower edge (a).

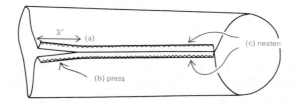

3″ (a)

(c) neaten

(b) press

(c) Fold sleeve RS together and stitch seam to this point. Fasten off well.

(d) Press seam open, including turnings below the opening (b). Neaten raw edges from end to end (c).

(e) Cut Wundaweb in half lengthwise and slip under edges of opening. Press well.

(f) Place RS cuff to RS sleeve edge. Pin front level with marked turning (d), but pin back to where underlap is marked (e).

At this stage make sure you are making a pair and not one sleeve that will wrap the wrong way.

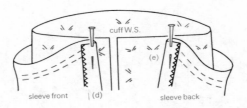

(g) Pull up gathers to fit (easier with gathers outside and cuff inside sleeve). Tack, machine, remove gathering threads.

(h) Press all turnings into cuff. Trim turnings down with medium scissors.

(i) Fold in all other edges $\frac{5}{8}$ in./15 mm, tack and press (f). Fold cuff on chalk mark, tack (g).

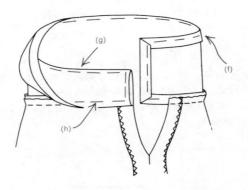

(j) With WS of sleeve towards you, bring cuff to meet machining and tack (h). Hem into machining, slip-stitch ends and overlap as for waistband (see pages 69–70).

(k) Slip sleeve on, fasten over to back and pin. Sew two press-studs size 0 or 00 (see page 60) to fasten.

Note: This opening comes under the arm so do not sew buttons there but put sleeve on and if you wish, sew two buttons in line with your little finger.

The easiest wrist finish of all

This is the elastic finish, which is very simple. You can adapt a pattern with a cuff to this finish. (See Designing for Beginners, page 92).

Requirements: Length of ¼ in./6 mm wide elastic, sufficient for both wrists, not too tight, plus ½ in./13 mm for each join.

Method

Follow hem method on page 50 for turning up a single machined hem until you reach the stage of doing the second row of machining.

(a) Set machine to straight stitch, small zigzag or blind stitch, or even for that matter, any other fancy stitch. Start at the underarm seam, work from RS if you can, reverse machine to start firmly then machine round sleeve (a). Stop ¾ in./20 mm from where you started and reverse again. This leaves a gap through which a safety pin can pass (b). Press well.

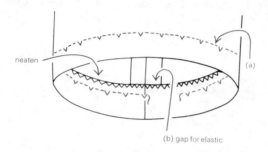

(b) gap for elastic

(b) Put a safety pin into one end of elastic. Thread elastic into sleeve. Remove pin. Overlap by ½ in./13 mm and join firmly with buttonhole stitch for strength (see page 62).

Stitch up the gap if you wish, although it is useful for adjusting or renewing the elastic, or removing it for washing.

Pressing cuffs and sleeves

Press cuff flat on WS then RS. Roll a towel into a sausage and slip into sleeve. Press sleeve with cuff to left running toe of iron into gathers but not over them. Pull cuff taut with left hand and slide iron point in and out.

19. Buttonholes

There are two types that beginners can manage: machine-made or piped. Both types must always be interfaced for strength down that section of the garment.

Machine-made buttonholes

Work last on the garment.

1. Mark positions very carefully with chalk, drawing a line down the garment to mark the centre front or forward end of the buttonhole (a). Draw a second line parallel with this the correct distance away, i.e. the diameter of the button+the thickness of the button+ $\frac{1}{8}$ in./3 mm for ease (b). Then draw horizontal lines to mark the buttonhole positions (c).

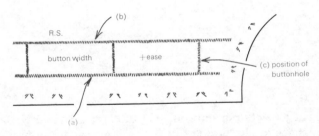

2. It helps to press a strip of Wundaweb between the two layers of fabric, in addition to interfacing, to prevent fraying later. Baste together the top layer, interfacing and facing.

3. Work the buttonholes according to the instructions in your machine handbook.

Pressing

Remove all tackings and press well before cutting the buttonholes.

Piped buttonholes

Work the first stage as early as possible.

This involves making a piping and stitching it through the garment, interfacing and Wundaweb only; the facing is used afterwards to neaten the back. Work each stage on all of the buttonholes at once.

1. Prepare chalk lines as described for machine buttonholes.

2. Make the strips of piping by cutting a long piece of fabric on the straight grain 2 in./5 cm wide. You will need at least 2 in./5 cm for each side of each buttonhole, or more if buttons are very large. A 12 in./30 cm strip therefore will make three buttonholes.

3. Press Bondaweb to WS strip. Remove paper when cool.

4. Fold strip in half lengthwise to form a 1 in./2·5 cm piping and press well until the Bondaweb seals it together. Trim piping to about ¼ in./6 mm wide, a little more on thick materials.

5. Cut piping into 2 in./5 cm or more, lengths. Place two pieces of piping against each chalked buttonhole with raw edges closely together (a). Tack pipings (b). Oversew the raw edges together if they tend to move apart.

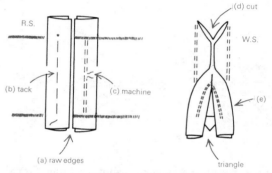

6. You are now ready to machine each piping in position. You are working a row of stitching exactly down the centre of each piping to give a fold-over of ⅛ in./3 mm for the finished buttonhole, so the stitching must be accurately parallel and the lines must be exactly the same length (sew by hand if you lack confidence). You have the chalk marks to give you the length so extend these right across the pipings so that you can see them when you machine. You also have the piping cut exactly to ¼ in./6 mm so you know you must keep to the middle.

7. Lower the machine needle into the centre of the piping, lower the foot and machine to end chalk mark, leaving needle in work, raise foot, turn work, lower foot and machine exactly on the previous stitching, proceeding to the chalk mark at the opposite end. Leave needle in work, lift foot, turn work, lower foot, and stitch back to centre (c). Remove and cut thread. This procedure gives the added strength of two rows of stitching and also means that you can

cut off the machine threads instead of sewing them in and having a weak point at each end of the buttonhole.

8. Remove all tackings. Press both sides of work.

9. To cut the buttonholes turn work to WS and snip, through garment only, the centre exactly between the two rows of stitching using small scissors. Then cut out towards the four ends of stitching to form a V (d). Cut right to the machine stitch, the Wundaweb prevents any fraying.

10. Push the pipings through the cut (e). They will pop through easily without any manipulating.

11. Tack just off the edge of the piping to hold flat (f). Push under triangles at each end using a pin. Press well on both sides.

12. On right side stab stitch by hand across the ends to hold triangles back (g).

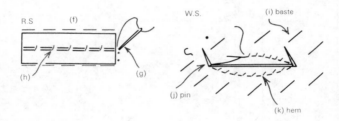

13. Oversew the piped edges, using tacking thread, to hold together (h).

14. Complete the garment.

Finishing off the wrong side

Having completed the rest of the garment as far as possible, and working on WS baste the facing to the section with the buttonholes worked, stitching round each buttonhole area to hold in place (i).

Turn to RS and plunge a pin (j) through each end of the buttonhole aperture. Turn to WS and snip carefully between the pins.

Hem by tucking the raw edge under a little way, using your needle, and work very tiny close stitches (k). Work a bar tack for strength across the end. On thicker fabrics it is better to cut a slit; and angle the ends exactly as you did when cutting the buttonhole because you then have more to turn under and it forms a rectangle similar to the one of the RS

Pressing

Press buttonholes well on both sides. Give the whole garment its final press and finally remove the oversewing.

20. Pockets

Avoid them if you can, but if you need one to use, or you want to balance a figure problem, use patch pockets. The other types of pocket are cut and should be ignored for quite a time yet.

If your pattern shows a pocket in a seam such as you may find in trousers, you should be able to cope with it by following the pattern instructions, but if you are at all nervous, leave them out, sewing the seam right up.

Patch pockets

The pattern will include a pocket piece but before cutting in fabric, cut one in a piece of odd fabric or interfacing and pin it to the garment. Move it around and make sure it is in a flattering position for you (for example, if you are short, you will have to raise them) and also make sure they will be a good size for your figure and not too overpowering.

Requirements

Light-weight interfacing. Iron-on is easiest, but try it first to make sure it works on your material. Lining, cotton lawn, or another piece of fabric if very light.

1. Cut out pockets in fabric, interfacing and interlining or backing.
2. Iron interfacing (or baste) to WS pockets.
3. Replace pattern and tailor tack turnings.
4. Remove pattern, turn in three edges of pocket, omitting top edge, on tailor tacks, tacking $\frac{1}{8}$ in./3 mm in from edge (a). Press edge only carefully.
5. If pocket has rounded corners you will find fullness at that point, snip the turnings and you will find it will lie flat (b).

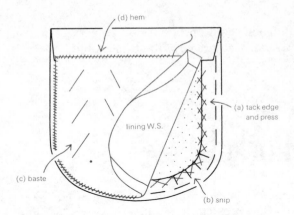

6. Use herringbone stitch to hold edges down. If fabric is light weight omit herringbone stitch and instead cut some very tiny pieces of Wundaweb and slip under the edge.

7. Turn down top edge of pocket. Cut Wundaweb to depth of top hem. Press. Slip Wundaweb underneath, press well. Remove tacking, press again.

8. Place lining or backing WS down to WS pocket and baste in position (c).

9. Work round pocket, turning in and tacking lining edge. Take it ⅛ in./3 mm back round three edges, but at least ½ in./13 mm tack along top edge. Hem lining to pocket from WS (d). Remove tacks.

Pressing

Place an extra layer of blanket or towel on your board and press the pocket gently first on the WS and then RS. Allow to cool.

Attaching the patch pocket

Marking position

1. Having decided on the best position mark where the top edge comes with chalk, also mark the ends. If there are to be two symmetrical pockets on the garment mark both positions. This entails folding and pinning the garment down the centre front, pinning armholes or side seams together and pinning the area round the chalk mark.

2. Tailor tack along the chalk mark and the ends. You cannot avoid doing tailor tacks here as you need the mark on the RS.

3. Unpin and open out garment.

Placing in position

1. Place each pocket in position on RS and anchor with two pins.

2. Attach by basting round all four sides but not close to the edge or it will bubble.

Stitching

1. Lift edge of pocket and work slipstitch (see page 70) just under the edge. Take very small, very firm stitches. Alternatively, on thick fabric, stitch from WS as for attaching 'frogs' (see page 59).

2. Work a very tiny bar tack at each top corner for strength. This is exactly like a loop for a hook (page 62), but is barely $\frac{1}{8}$ in./3 mm long.

Pressing

Remove tacks. Place work RS down and press WS, then turn and press again on RS, this time over a towel.

21. Designing for Beginners

Making your own patterns is an advanced subject but even beginners can create styles for themselves by making simple alterations to existing patterns.

To start with alter only one small area and make sure not only that your fabric is of a suitable weight for the variation which you have in mind, but also that you have enough material to cut the new style.

A plain high neck can have a tie collar (a) attached instead of facings. See page 93 for the pattern.

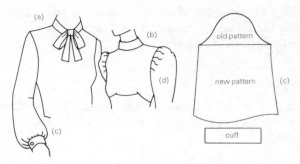

Another possibility for such a neckline is a shaped band collar (b) and sewing instructions can be found in the section on Collars on page 74.

Sleeve styles can be changed provided you keep the head of the sleeve the same so that it matches the armhole. For example, a plain sleeve can be changed by using a shirt sleeve pattern from the underarm down (c). An exception is a sleeve with a gathered head which can be used to replace a plain sleeve entirely (d).

Almost any neckline can be finished with a double bind and a bow (e) as described on page 62. This works particularly well with jersey fabrics.

A shirt sleeve can be adapted to a sleeve without a cuff (f) by cutting the pattern across and inserting 3 in./7·5 cm of extra paper. The bottom of the sleeve is then gathered into the wrist with elastic. See page 84.

For fine fabrics a frilled cuff (g) can be achieved by inserting 5 in./12·5 cm and trimming the bottom of the pattern straight across. This edge is finished with a very narrow hem and a 1 in./2·5 cm strip cut to make a casing for a narrow elastic. This is machined to the WS of the sleeve 3 in./7·5 cm up from the bottom.

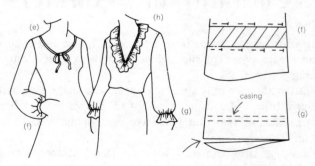

A 'V' neck can be decorated with a double frill in a fine material and neatened with a double bind (h). For the frill cut a strip on the straight grain $5\frac{1}{2}$ in./14 cm wide and three times longer than the neckline. Fold in half lengthwise, RS together, and stitch across the ends (CB). Trim and turn to right side and baste the layers together. Run gathering threads $\frac{1}{2}$ in./13 mm in from the raw edge and pin frill to neckline, pulling up gathers to fit. Machine and then finish edge with a double bind (see page 52).

A deep frill can look good on a skirt (i). Hold the pattern of a long plain skirt up to you and, standing in front of a mirror, decide on a depth for the frill which will give a good proportion for your height.

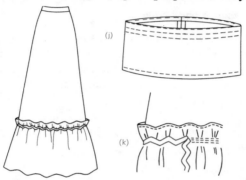

Trim off bottom of pattern on this line, adding a $\frac{5}{8}$ in./15 mm turning. Cut a length of fabric to the depth of the frill plus $1\frac{1}{2}$ in./3·8 cm and at least three times longer than the edge of the skirt to which it will be attached. Seam the short ends together and press open. Turn in a narrow hem on each long edge and run two gathering threads $\frac{3}{4}$ in./2 cm down from the top edge (j). Pin WS of frill to RS of skirt, pull up gathers to fit and tack and machine. The machine stitching can be covered with a decorative braid if desired (k).

Pattern for tie collar

Cut two pieces of fabric on straight grain 27 in./68·5 cm long by $4\frac{1}{2}$ in./11·5 cm wide. Mark $\frac{5}{8}$ in./15 cm turnings all round each piece and a centre fold line with chalk – see Collar (a).

Collar (a)

$\longleftarrow$ ———————— 27"/68.5 cm ———————— $\longrightarrow$

$4\frac{1}{2}$"

11.5 cm

Collar (b)   1 sq.=1″/2.5 cm   ⅝″/1.5 cm. turnings allowed

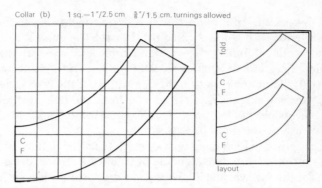

Pattern for shaped band collar

Copy collar on to paper divided into 1 in./2·5 cm squares (Collar b).
Trace off or cut out the pattern and check by placing against neckline.
If necessary the pattern can be lengthened or shortened at CB, and
one end can be extended to give an underlap. Cut out twice with CF
placed to a fold – see layout.

Appendix

Useful addresses

Aero Zips Ltd, Aero House, Ealing Road, Wembley, Middlesex, make and distribute zip fasteners throughout the UK.

Bogod Machine Co. Ltd, 50–2 Great Sutton Street, London, EC1, UK distributors for the range of Bernina Sewing Machines.

J. & P. Coats (UK) Ltd, Central Office, 12 Seedhill Road, Paisley, PA1 1JP. Manufacturers of Drima multi-purpose sewing thread.

Creative Features Ltd, 2a, High Street, Redhill, Surrey, supply paper patterns by post.

Elna Sewing Machines (GB) Ltd, Queens House, 180–2 Tottenham Court Road, London W1P 0HY. Distributors of Elna Sewing Machines.

English Sewing Ltd, PO Box 245, 56 Oxford Street, Manchester M60 1HL, make Sylko and Trylko Sewing threads.

Lightning Fastners Ltd, Kynoch Works, Witton, Birmingham B6 7BA, make Lightning and Optilon zip fasteners.

Needle Industries Ltd, Studley, Warwickshire, make needles of all types and sewing aids.

Newey Goodman Ltd, Robin Hood Lane, Hall Green, Birmingham B28 0JG, make hooks and eyes and press studs and sewing aids.

H. W. Peel & Co. Ltd, Chartwell House, Jeymer Drive, Greenford, Middlesex, produce True Sew squared pattern paper.

Perivale-Gutermann Ltd, Wandsworth Road, Greenford, Middlesex UB6 7JS. Manufacturers of Gutermann Polyester and Polyester Twist, and Gutermann Silk and Silk Twist.

Pfaff (Britain) Ltd, 22 Croydon Street, Domestic Industrial Estate, Leeds LS11 9RT. Distributors of Pfaff domestic sewing machines.

Selectus Ltd, Biddulph, Stoke-on-Trent, Staffordshire ST8 7RH, make Velcro fastener, petersham and ribbons.

Singer Co. (UK) Ltd, 255 High Street, Guildford, Surrey GU1 3DH, distribute Singer machines throughout the UK.

Vilene Ltd, Greetland, Halifax, West Yorkshire HX4 8NJ, make Vilene, Wundaweb, and Bondaweb. A booklet *Guide to Dressmaking with Vilene* is available and Vilene also run an Information Service.

Books

McCalls Sewing in Colour, published by Paul Hamlyn.
Simplicity Sewing Books, published by Simplicity.
The Vogue Sewing Book, published by Vogue Patterns.
Everything about Sewing Series, published by Vogue Patterns.
Golden Hands Encyclopaedia, published by Marshall Cavendish.
Specialist Dress Materials and their handling, by A. Catriona Kirby; published by McDonald.
Ladies' Coat and Skirt Making, by Samuel Heath, published by Crosby Lockwood.
Dress Pattern Designing, by Natalie Bray, published by Crosby Lockwood.

Lessons

1. There are classes in dressmaking in every area, run by the Local Authority.
2. Residential weekends in dressmaking are held at various Adult Short-course colleges.
3. Free or cheap sewing lessons are available at some sewing machine centres.

Index

Compiled by S. Kennedy

Italics refer to extended references